Discover Your Europe

Berlin Central Station (Germany)

InfoRailMap Country Index
Flag, Country name and page number(s)

A
- Albania 27, 40
- Algeria 19
- Austria 23, 53 56 62 63 55 58 64 65

B
- Belgium 11, 20
- Bosnia 40
- Bulgaria 44, 45

C
- Corsica 24
- Croatia 38, 40
- Czechia 36, 38, 57

D
- Denmark 34

E
- England 6, 8

F
- Finland 29, 31
- France 10, 12, 20, 50

G
- Germany 20, 22, 52
- Greece 44, 46

H
- Hungary 38, 39, 65

I
- Iceland 28
- Ireland 3
- Italy 22, 24, 26, 50 54 60

L
- Lithuania 66
- Luxembourg 20
- Liechtenstein 22, 52

M
- Macedonia 41
- Montenegro 40
- Morocco 18

N
- Netherlands 20
- Norway 28, 32

P
- Poland 35, 37
- Portugal 16, 18

R
- Romania 42, 43

S
- Sardinia 24
- Scotland 4, 5
- Serbia 38, 40
- Sicily 26
- Slovakia 38, 39, 63
- Slovenia 38, 61
- Spain 12, 14, 16, 18
- Sweden 28, 30, 32, 34
- Switzerland 22, 48 49 52

T
50 51 54
- Tunisia 15, 26
- Turkey 45, 47

A-Z of major tourist destinations are listed on page 67.

ISBN: 978-1-911165-41-5

Published by Solitaire Contracts Limited. All text, graphics, RailMaps, icons, info graphics, photographs, RailMap Logo and Cover design © **2020 Solitaire Contracts Limited**. All rights reserved. No part of this publication by whatever technology or device may be rendered or reproduced in order to be printed or displayed in any way or form or in any location in any part of the world. **InfoRailMap** is a graphic artefact and basic schematic representation of the European railway network and is **not to physical scale**, does **not include all station stops** or include every town that has significant cultural or historic value.

Complimentary PDF info can be found on page 14 and by visiting InfoRailMap.com

InfoRailMap Legend - Discover all the major tourist locations

- 🔴 **Capital city**
- ⚫ **Provincial City**
- ⚪ **Provincial Town**
- 🟣 **Border Town**
- ⌐ **Boarder**

Capital cities are identified by extra large red dot and city name highlighted.
Top tourist destinations and major transport hubs are highlighted by a **black dot**. **Station stops** between the major towns and cities are indicated by a smaller grey dots. Not all station stops are included.
Boarder towns are indicated by a purple dot. **Country boarders** are indicated by brown highlighted lines. In Eastern Europe expected to have your passport checked.

- ━●━ **Icons** 🏛🏰 **Bold [location name]**
- ━●━ **Location stop only** TGV, IC, AV etc ...
- 🚂 **Steam train** Private train NB. Not included in Railpass

Important **tourist rich locations** are identified with **bigger black dot** and **icons**. The larger the icons the more significant the attraction. **Important locations** where intercity fast trains typically stop eg **TGV, Thalys, ES, AV, Eurostar** etc which always require additional supplements and/or seat reservation and are indicated by orange line and black dot. **Private railways and seasonal routes** are included with the little steam train icon. For example the seasonal **Swedish Inlandsbanan** and **Scarborough Spa Express** in **England**. Open all year are the Zillertalbahn private railway between Jenback ↔ Mayrhofen (Austria) and the Jacobite steam train (Scotland) between Mallaig ↔ Fort William.

Railway/Bus/Ferry/S-Bahn network

- ━━━ **TGV, IC, AV, TLK, EST** *(Compulsory supp / seat res)*
- ━━━ **ICE, RJ** (Germany, Austria) *(NO Supp / seat res required)*
- ━━━ **Mainline railway line**
- ━━━ **Local railway line**
- ━━━ **Scenic route**
- ━━━ **Tourist Route** (Private) *(Compulsory supp / seat res)*
- ━━━ **S-Bahn**
- ┄┄┄ **Railway Tunnel**
- 🚌 **Bus Route**
- ━━━ **Ferry Route**
- 🚢 **Cruise Ship**
- ⛴ **Passenger Ferry**
- ⛵ **Sailing boats**

All high speed routes eg **TGV, Thalys, AV, ES, InterCity (IC)** and **EuroCity (EC)** are connected by orange lines and require mandatory supps/seat res. The **Interrail App** always indicates where supps and seat res are **compulsory**.

High-speed German **ICE/IC** and Austrian **RJ/IC/EC** Routes are indicated by purples lines are included in RailPass. **Always** check if seat is reserved which is indicated by the electronic display located above or side of the seat.

All other connections between cities, unless indicated above, are mainline. Always double check the **Interrail App** before boarding especially in **Eastern Europe** and **Greece**. NB: **Polish TLK** reservations are free.

Local regional lines ie **RE/R/TER** etc in every country are completely free to travel on. Regional trains usually take different, more interesting, routes than fast main line ones. Especially in **Austria, Germany** and **Italy**.

Many of the scenic routes are absolutely jaw dropping spectacular and are indicated by bright green highlight.

Privately run scenic routes typically in **Austria** (Jenbach ↔ Mayhofen) and dedicated trains/carriages in **Switzerland eg** (Glacier Express) do require additional tickets and are indicated by green highlighted line.

All **S-Bahn** (not **U-Bahn**) trains (**Austria, Switzerland** and **Germany**) are included in RailPass. Many Airports in **Germany** are connected to **S-Bahn** (NB. Green logo signs - blue on **InfoRailMap**). NB: Always remember to complete railpass travel diary.

Railway tunnels are present in most countries. EC/IC fast train services between Visp ↔ Spiez is through **Gottard Base Tunnel** and misses all the beautiful scenery!

Bus routes are indicated by thin pink lines. **Swiss Travel Pass** includes bus and railway services.

Europe contains many stunning islands and ferry connections are abundant particularly in **Scandinavia, UK, Ireland, Greece, Mediterranean Sea** and for getting to and from **North Africa**. For many locations ferries (large, small, fast and slow) are the only way to get there without flying. Don't let having to arrange a ferry deter you from visiting **Finland, Sardinia, Corsica, Malta** or **Greek islands** for example. It is super easy to arrange online and ports are always easy to get to via public transport. Due to the lack of space only a selection of popular ferry connections are included. Always check Interrail App for potential discounts as they change yearly and discounts also change seasonally. Many popular routes attract huge discounts so well worth checking out. Websites info is included for the most popular routes which attract railpass discounts.

InfoRailMap Icons

- 🏛 **UNESCO site** Roman artifact, Protected landscape
- 🏰 **Castle, Fort,** Bridge, Cittadelle
- ⛪ **Religious building** Cathedral, Mosque, Monastery, Abbey
- 🏠 **Historic town** Old world buildings, Museums eg Altstadt
- 🛡 **Medieval buldings** Preserved buildings ie fresco artwork

The bigger the icon for the main tourist destination denotes the bigger and more attractive the location.

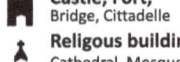 **Horse racing**

 **Shower facilities**

 **Airport CODE**

 **Luggage store**

 **Spa, Wellness**

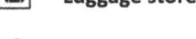

 **Gastronomy** Beer, Coffee, Food

InfoRailMap 2020 icons clearly identify **UNESCO** sites, important monuments and protected landscapes, historically important **Roman artefacts**, religiously inspired buildings including **cathedrals, mosques, monasteries, abbeys** and **interesting churches**. Also significant and well worth stopping off to admire are the numerous **castles** *(name/attraction)*, **châteaux, forts, bridges and citadels**. Unique to Europe are it's stunning **old world medieval towns** many of which are lovingly restored, preserved and kept in tip top shape (notably in **Belgium, Italy, France, Czechia** and **Slovakia**) and being continually cleaned, rebuilt and improved in **Germany**. New for **2020** is the **Medieval icon** which denotes locations where buildings and significant **Romanesque**, and **Gothic** sites. For example buildings which have external **sgraffito/fresco** paintings and buildings from this era including **Switzerland, Austria** and **Germany** which display external artwork for instance **Lindau (Germany)** and **Feldkirch and Innsbruck (Austria)**. Thus is you have limited time the bigger icons are the most impressive locations to visit. For example **Toledo** (south of **Madrid**) in **Spain** is a magnificent display of the most impressive of all the icons.

InfoRailMap icons primarily indicate where to focus your attention if you want to speed tour the continent, however due to space (with the exception of the detailed **InfoRailMap** for **Switzerland/Austria/Northern Italy**) only provide info on the major towns and is in no way a definitive schematic of every single delightful old world town to visit.

Predominately in **England, Scotland, Ireland** and **France** is the popular sport of **horse racing** which is denoted with a race horse and is well worth the effort particularly in **Ireland** as racecourses always have ample facilities to sample the local beer and Guinness.

Budget airlines provide almost instant access to many top locations. Consider including budget airlines if you want to tour the whole continent with a global pass. Top destinations are work back from are **Portugal, Norway** and **Greece**.

The **luggage store** icon is only displayed in the **Switzerland** detailed **InfoRailMap** pages due to lack of space on the main **Map** pages. Although the majority of major train stations offer some kind of coin operated luggage store.

Food and alcohol have important cultural significance and where you can expect to find outdoor cafe/restaurant/beer culture the **Gastronomy** icon is displayed.

Discovering the awesome scenery

 **Mountain** Height meters

 **Funicular**

 **Ski slopes**

 **Ski lifts**

 **Hiking trails** Summer walking routes

 **Lakes, rivers**

 **Landscape**

 **Park, Forest**

🌟 **Scenic view**

Europe has a diverse climate and relevant icons display geographical info. Detailed **InfoRailMap** pages covering **Swiss, French, German** and **Italian Alps** include the **Mountain icon** and is accompanied with the elevation height in meters in order to get an accurate idea of what to expect. **Mont Blanc (4,810km)** in **France** is the highest peak in **Europe** closely followed by **Swiss Matterhorn (4,478km)**. **Swiss Jungfraujock (3,466km)** affectionately called the **"Top of Europe"** is actually the most attractive of extended mountain ranges and thus has an enormous purpose built viewing platform so you can admire the full scale of this wondrous and extra special location. Each country has a slightly different take on how each look after their green space. The **Hiking** icon is included with many towns and cities and indicates that walking is the best option for discovering the location.

2 **N**orthLink Ferries:
Scrabster ↔ Stromness (2.5 hrs)
(peak foot passenger £24.00).
Kirkwall ↔ Lerwick (8.5 hrs pm).
Winter 3 wkly. Summer 4 wkly.
(peak foot passenger £19.40).
www.northlinkferries.co.uk

Cruise Loch Lomond:
Tarbet ↔ Ulg, Lochmadddy etc.
Definitive list of all highland cruises.
www.cruiselochlomond.co.uk

Wallace monument (Scotland) can be clearly seen from **Sterling Castle**. To reach **Sterling castle** from Sterling train station head over the road for easy to read map for how to reach the tourist office and Castle (20 min walk). The Castle grounds and beautiful Cemetery opposite are completely free to explore.

Caledonian MacBrayne:
Oban ↔ Castlebay
Reg service. 5 hrs.
www.calmac.co.uk

Scottish Highlands: www.visitscotland.com
Learn more about all the ferry companies that service this stunning area of natural beauty and more about Scotland in general.

6 **J**acobite railway line:
Famous super scenic route
Mallaig ↔ Fort William.

Belfast (Northern Ireland) is a brilliant city to discover with the vast Titanic installation, castle, pubs and stunning scenery.

Frequent bus services connecting major cities in Scotland. citylink.co.uk

Irish Train Travel can be found at irishrail.ie

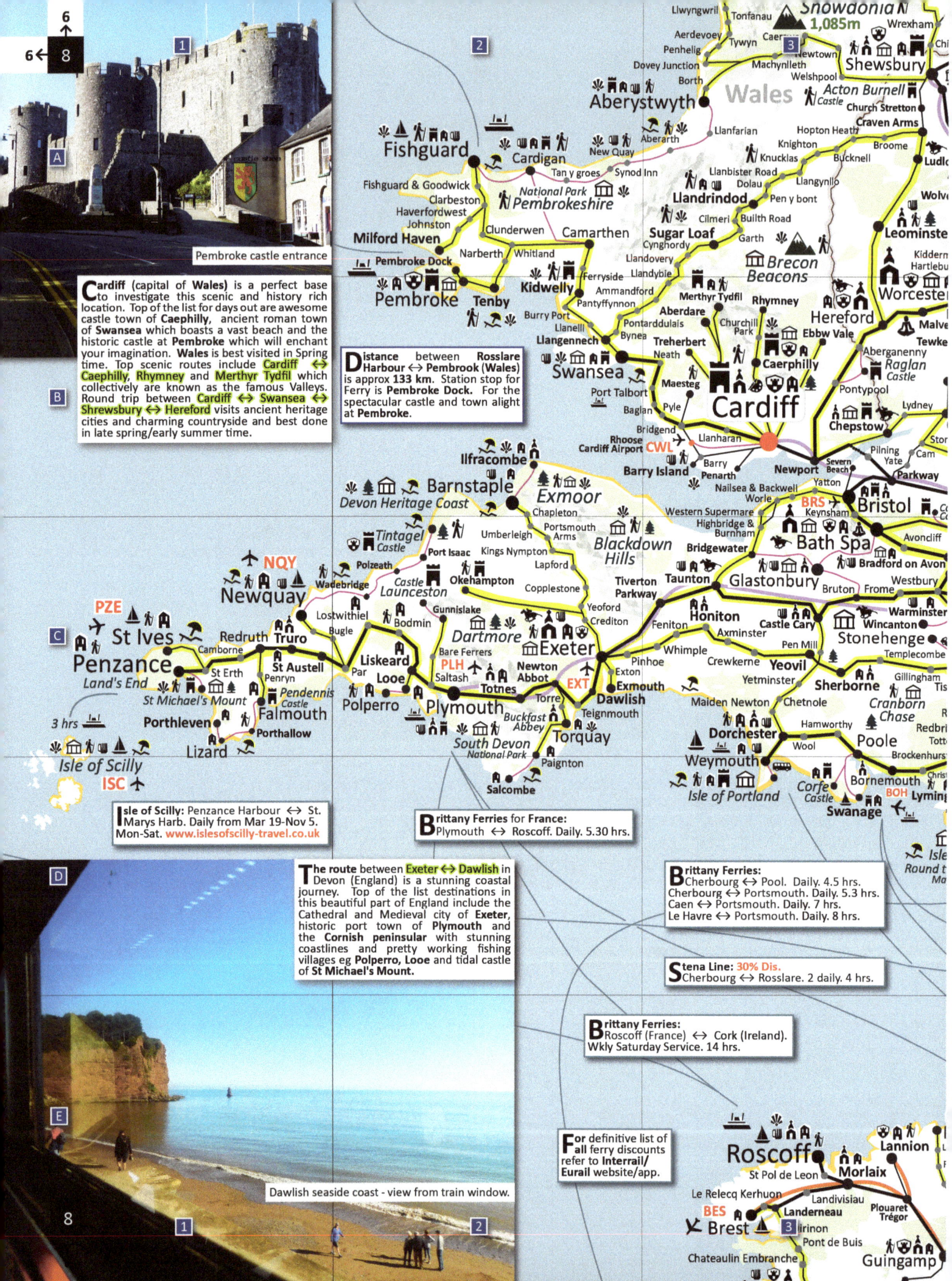

Pembroke castle entrance

Cardiff (capital of Wales) is a perfect base to investigate this scenic and history rich location. Top of the list for days out are awesome castle town of **Caephilly**, ancient roman town of **Swansea** which boasts a vast beach and the historic castle at **Pembroke** which will enchant your imagination. **Wales** is best visited in Spring time. Top scenic routes include **Cardiff ↔ Caephilly, Rhymney** and **Merthyr Tydfil** which collectively are known as the famous Valleys. Round trip between **Cardiff ↔ Swansea Shrewsbury ↔ Hereford** visits ancient heritage cities and charming countryside and best done in late spring/early summer time.

Distance between Rosslare Harbour ↔ Pembrook (Wales) is approx 133 km. Station stop for Ferry is **Pembroke Dock**. For the spectacular castle and town alight at **Pembroke**.

Isle of Scilly: Penzance Harbour ↔ St. Marys Harb. Daily from Mar 19-Nov 5. Mon-Sat. www.islesofscilly-travel.co.uk

The route between **Exeter ↔ Dawlish** in Devon (England) is a stunning coastal journey. Top of the list destinations in this beautiful part of England include the Cathedral and Medieval city of **Exeter**, historic port town of **Plymouth** and the **Cornish peninsular** with stunning coastlines and pretty working fishing villages eg **Polperro, Looe** and tidal castle of **St Michael's Mount**.

Dawlish seaside coast - view from train window.

Brittany Ferries for **France**:
Plymouth ↔ Roscoff. Daily. 5.30 hrs.

Brittany Ferries:
Cherbourg ↔ Pool. Daily. 4.5 hrs.
Cherbourg ↔ Portsmouth. Daily. 5.3 hrs.
Caen ↔ Portsmouth. Daily. 7 hrs.
Le Havre ↔ Portsmouth. Daily. 8 hrs.

Stena Line: **30% Dis.**
Cherbourg ↔ Rosslare. 2 daily 4 hrs.

Brittany Ferries:
Roscoff (France) ↔ Cork (Ireland).
Wkly Saturday Service. 14 hrs.

For definitive list of all ferry discounts refer to Interrail / Eurail website/app.

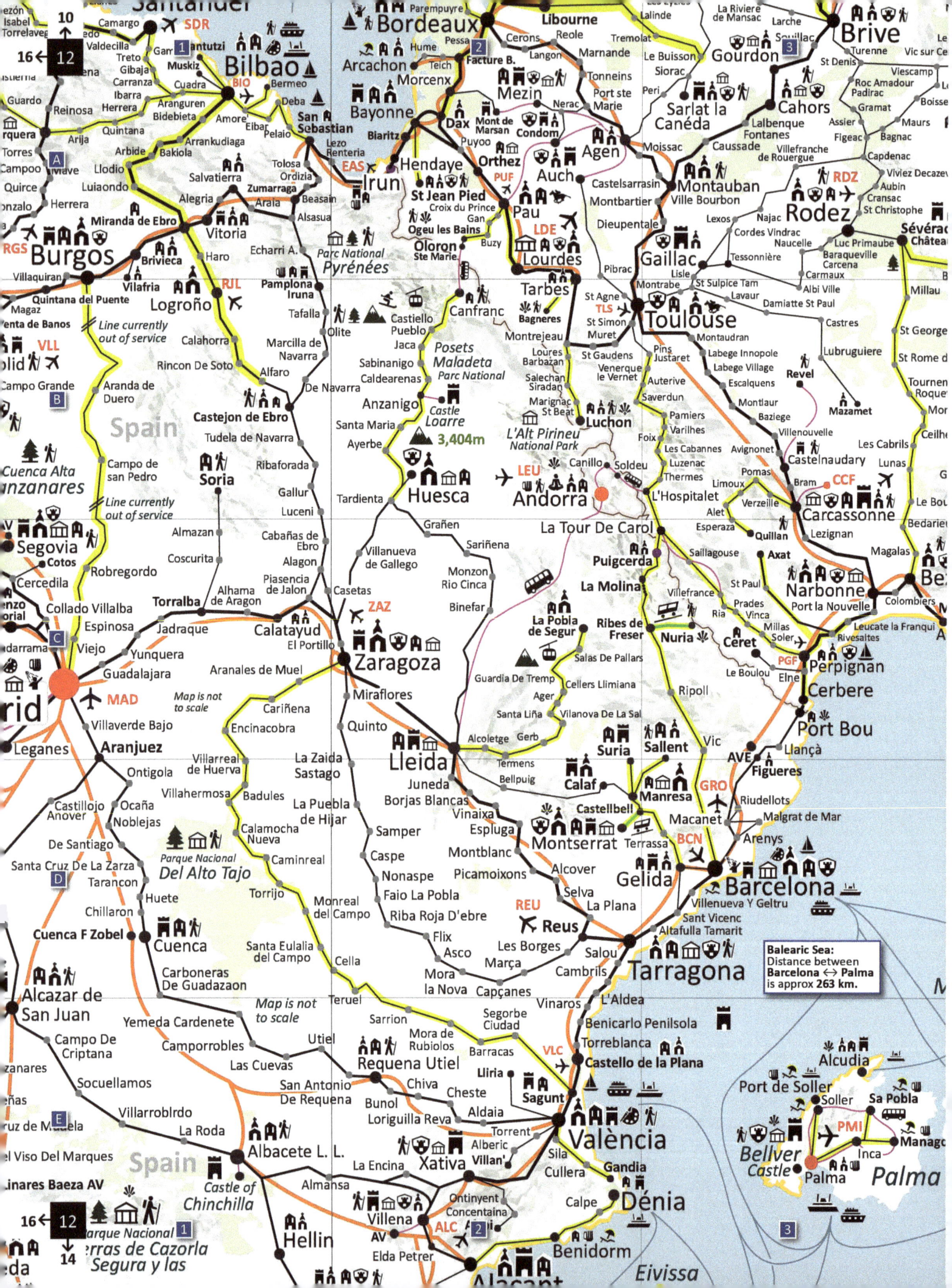

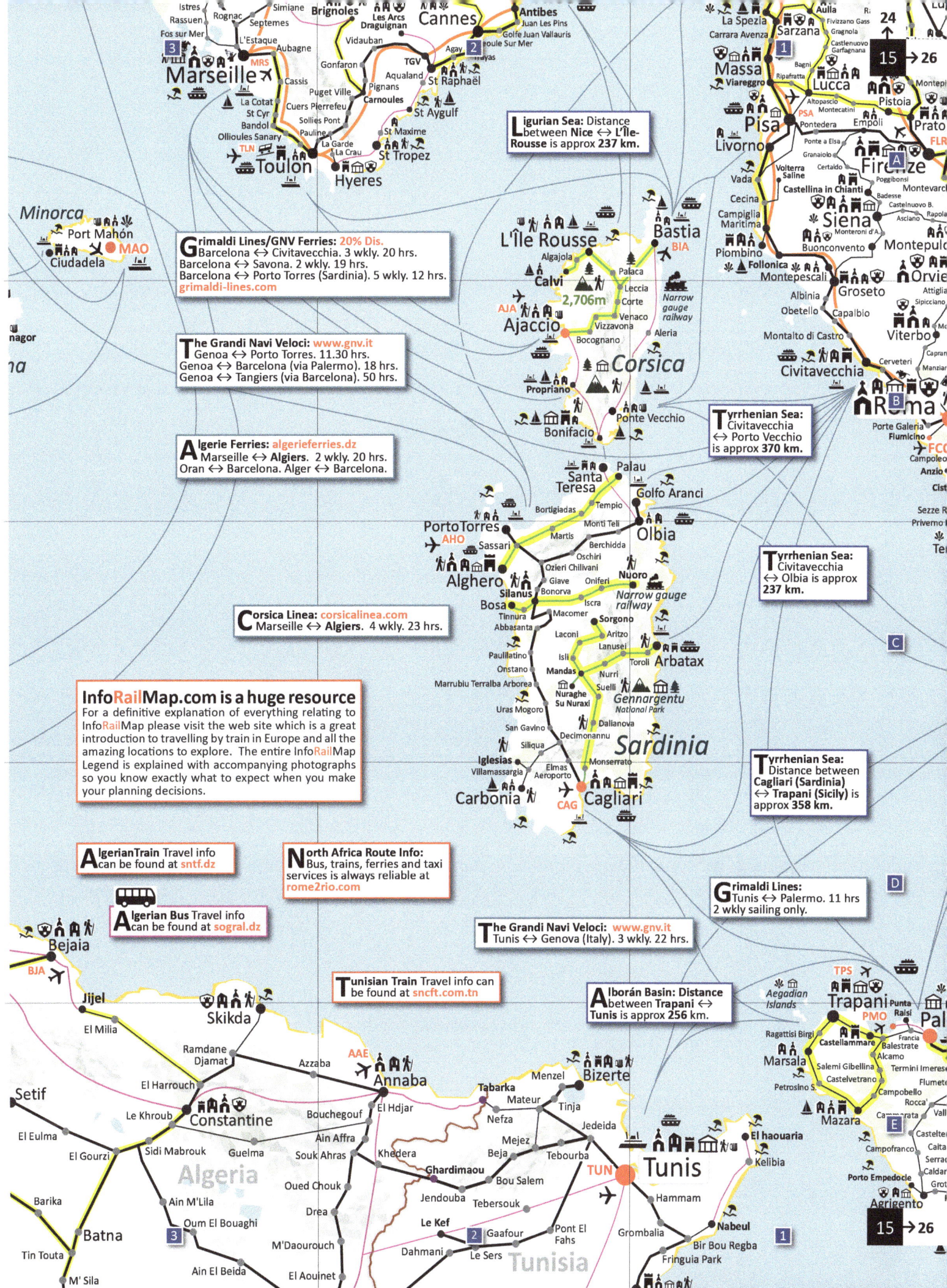

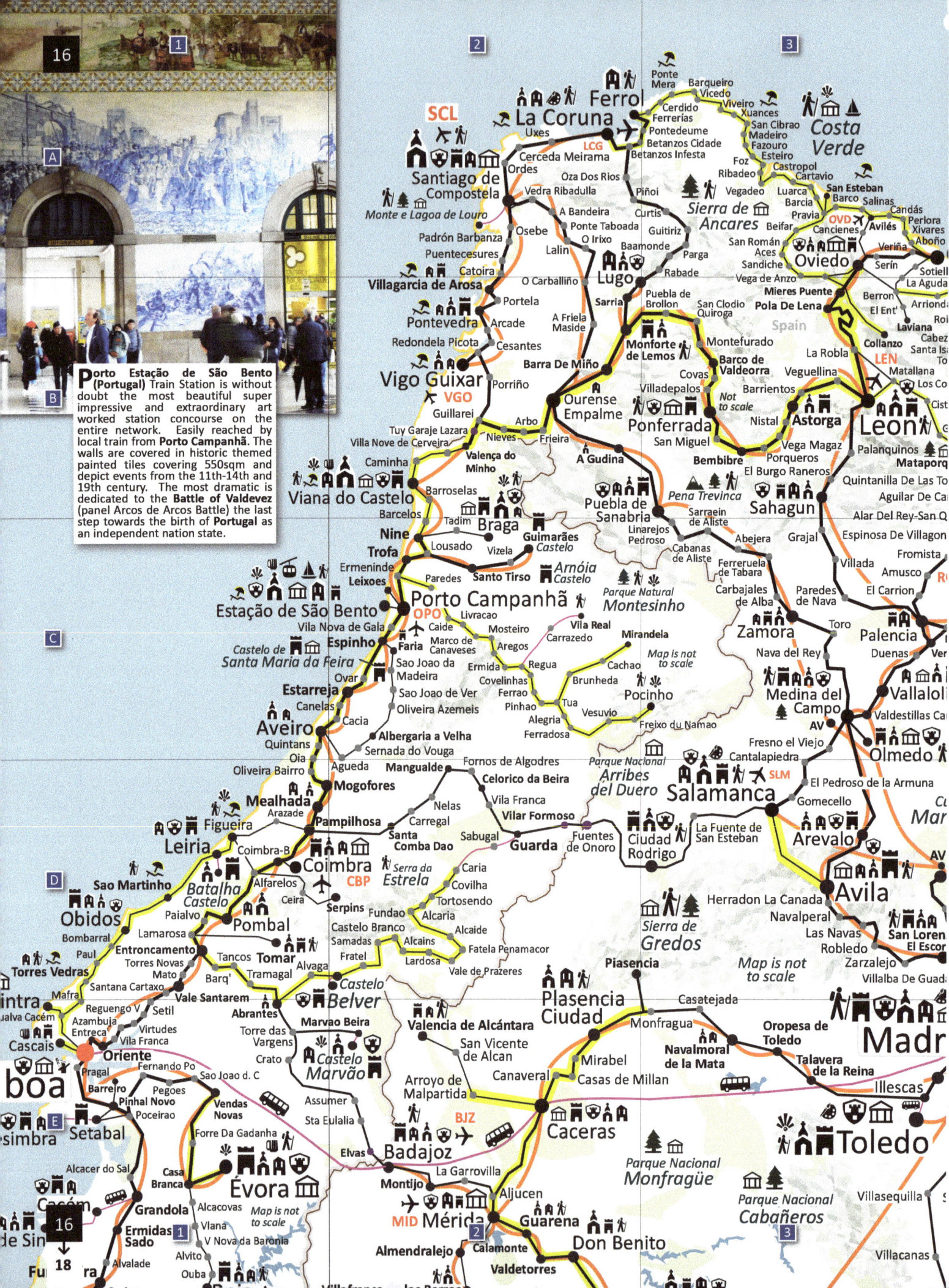

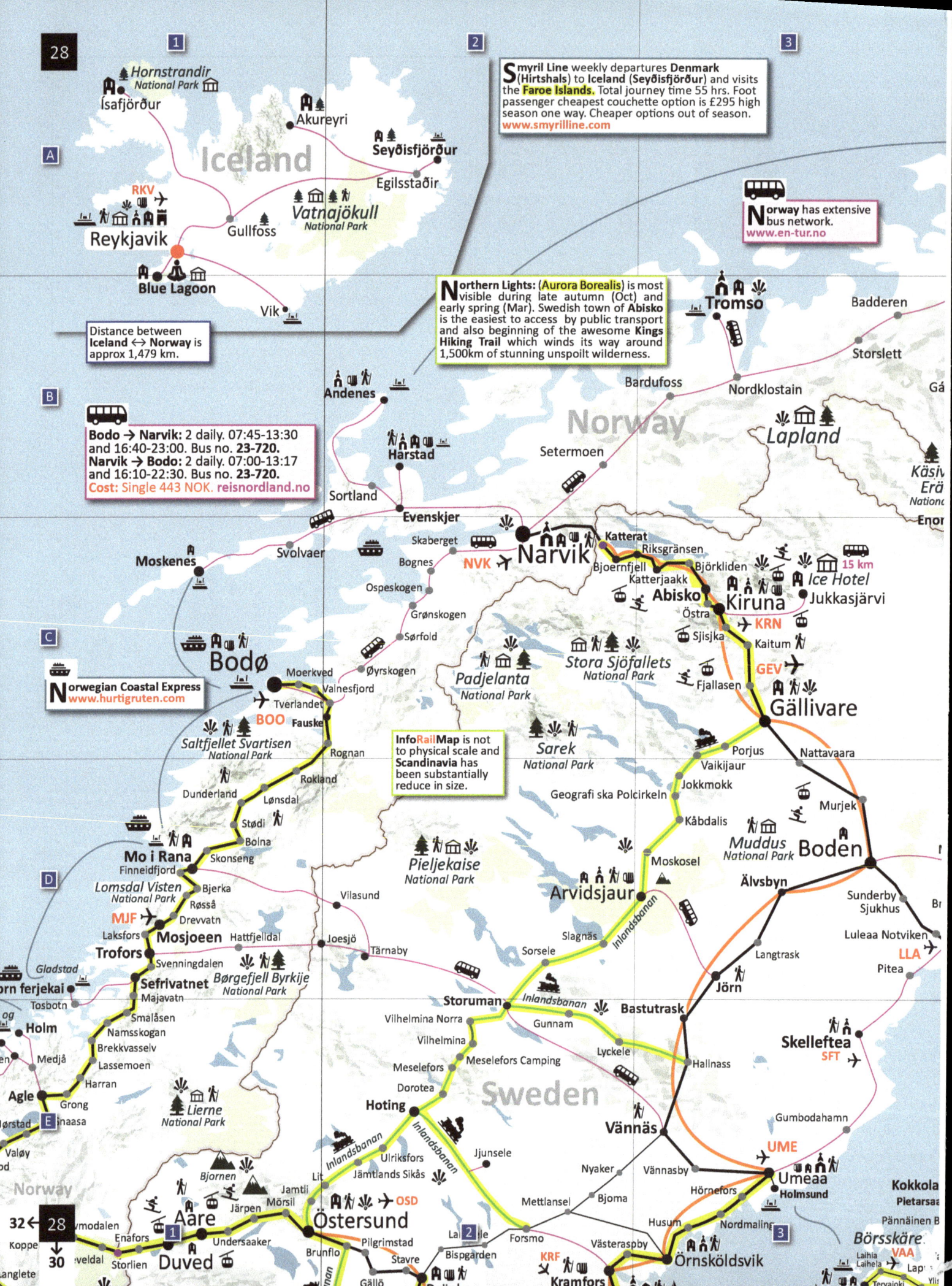

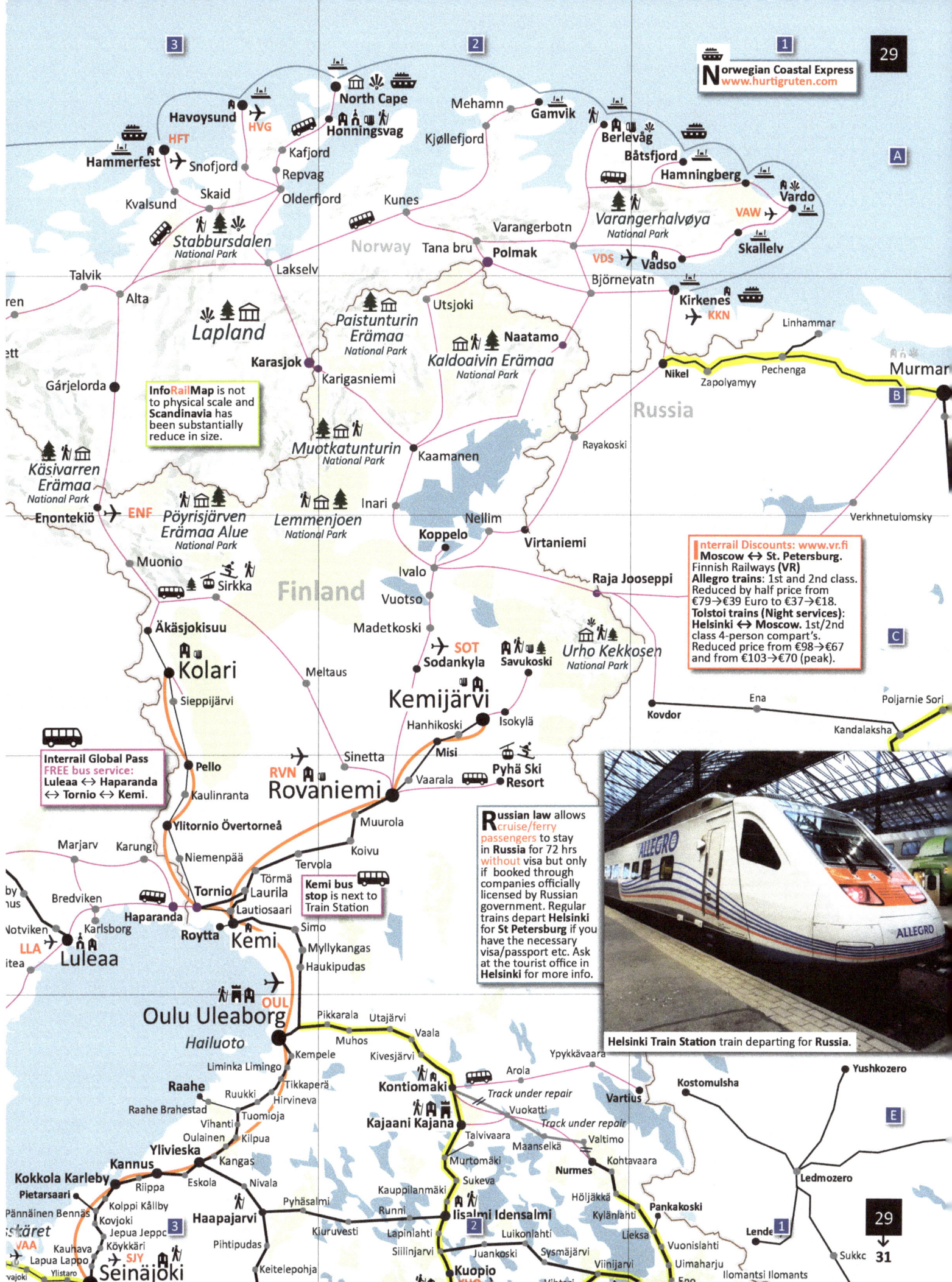

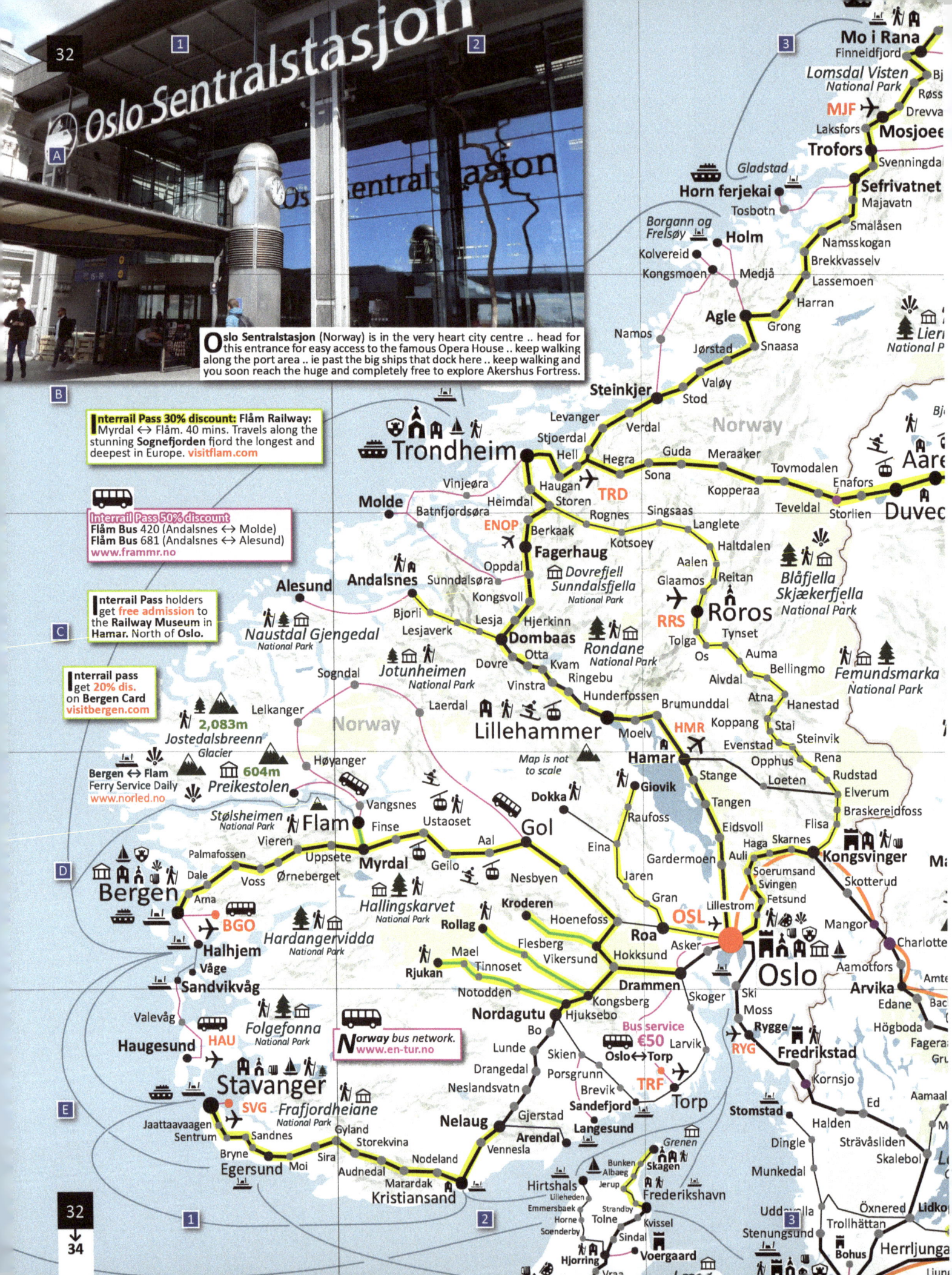

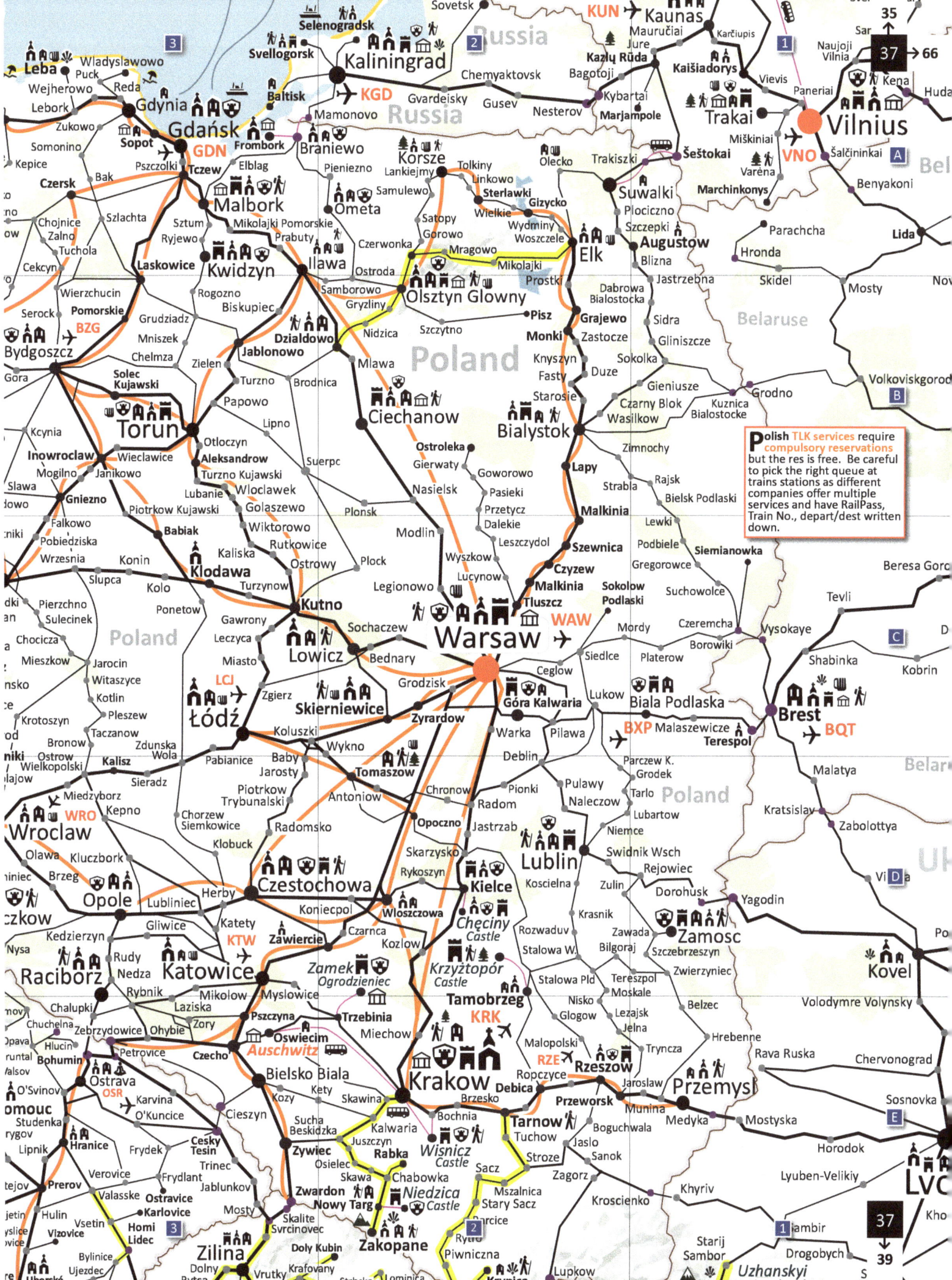

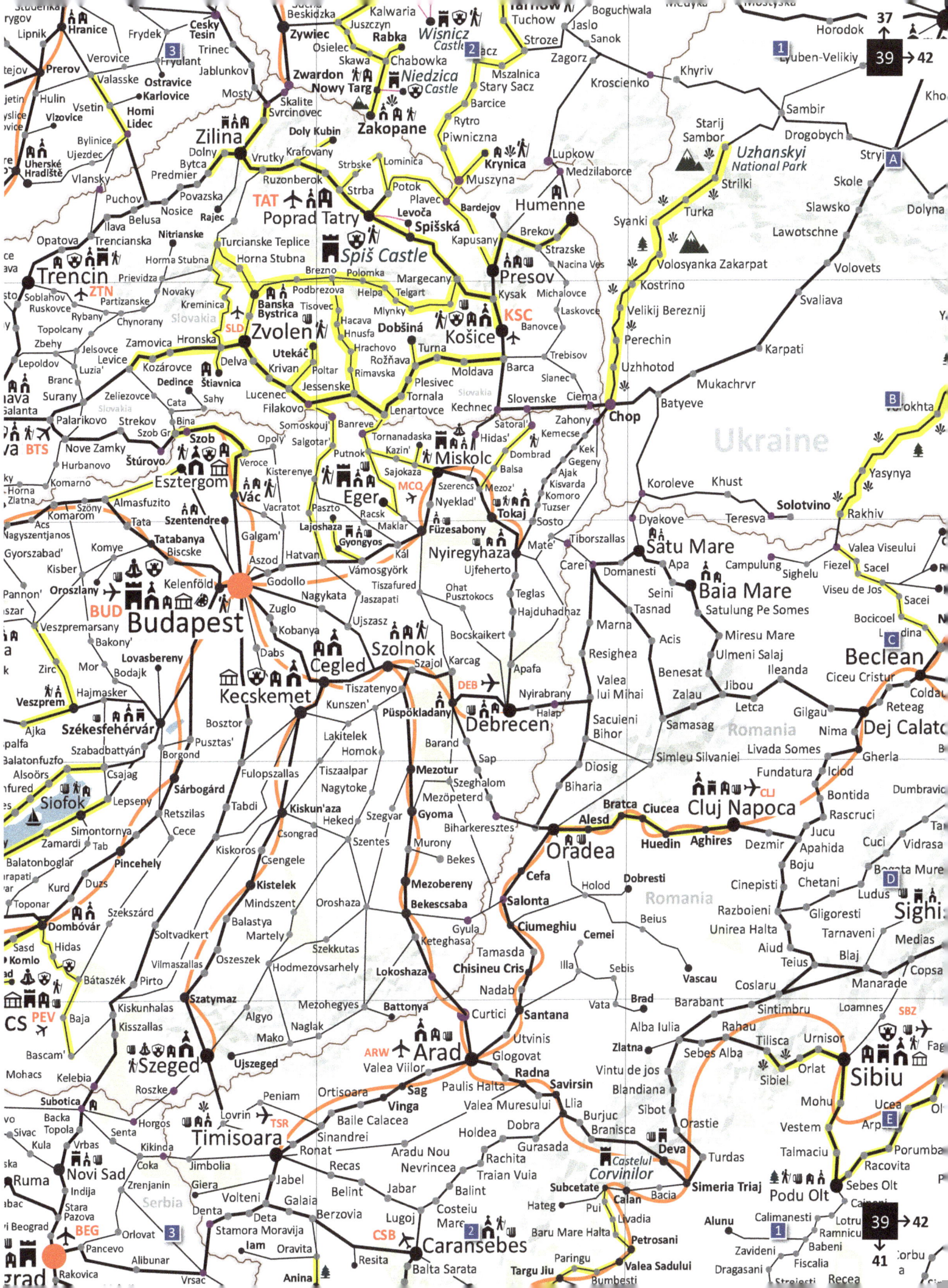

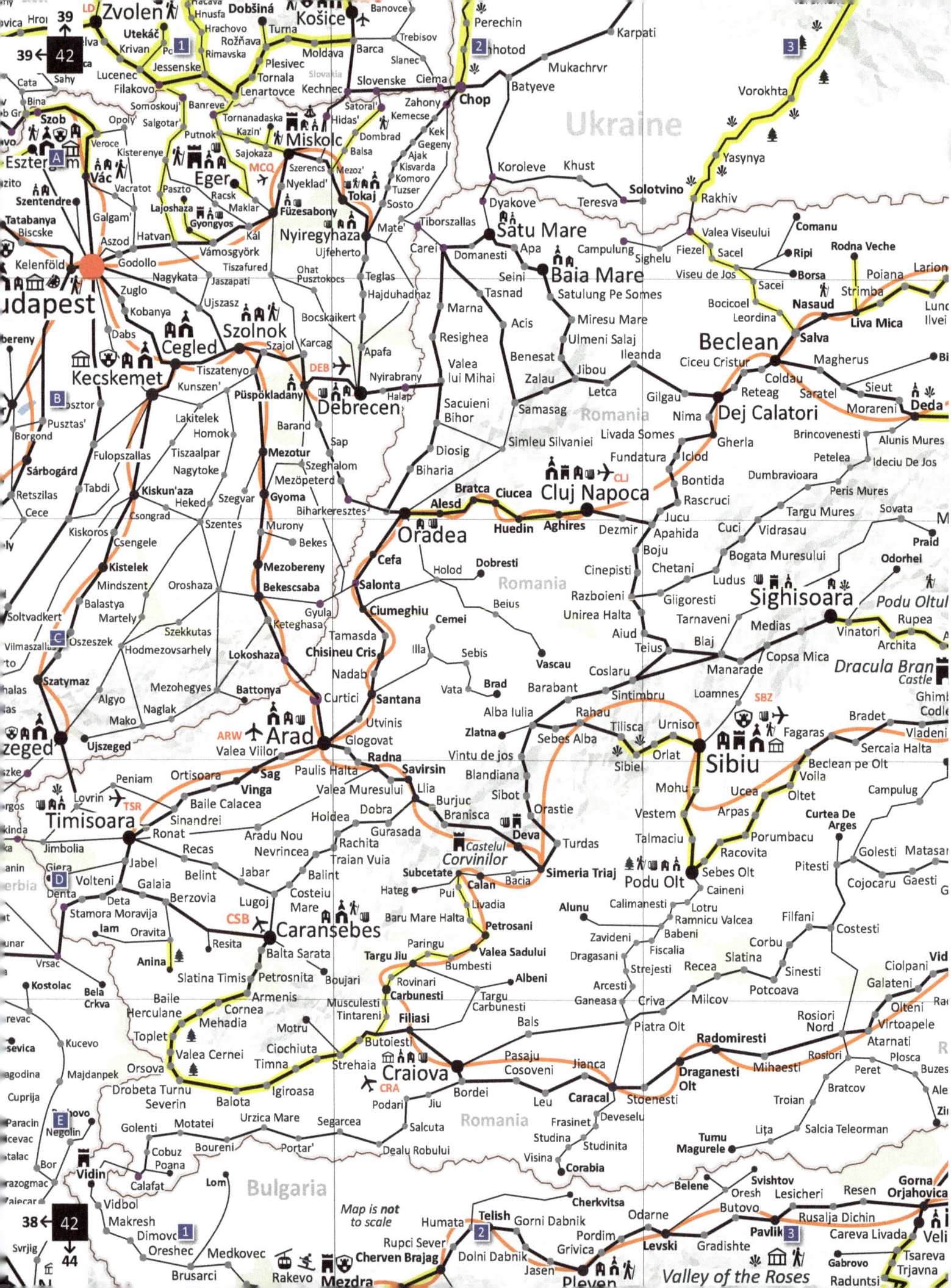

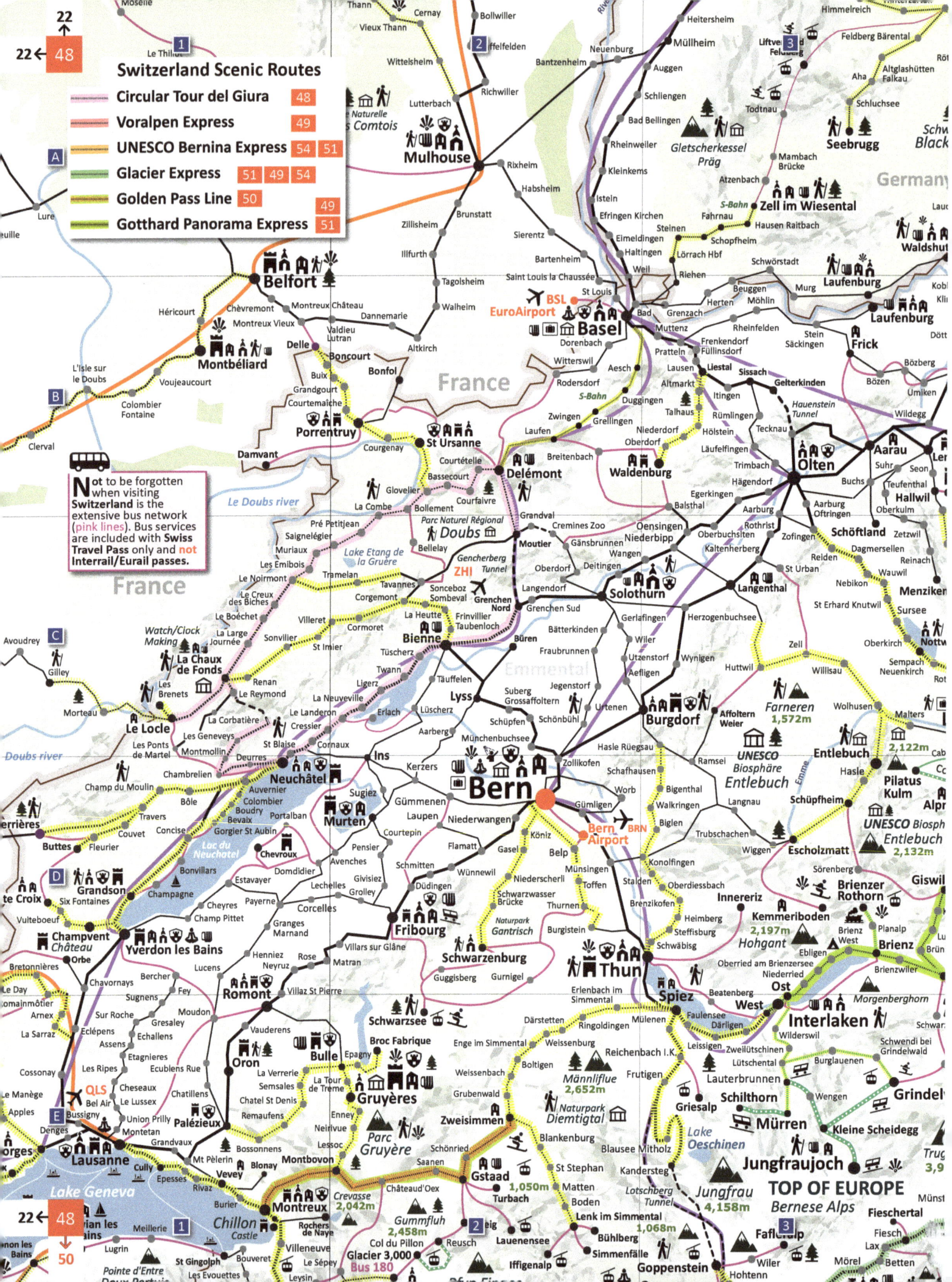

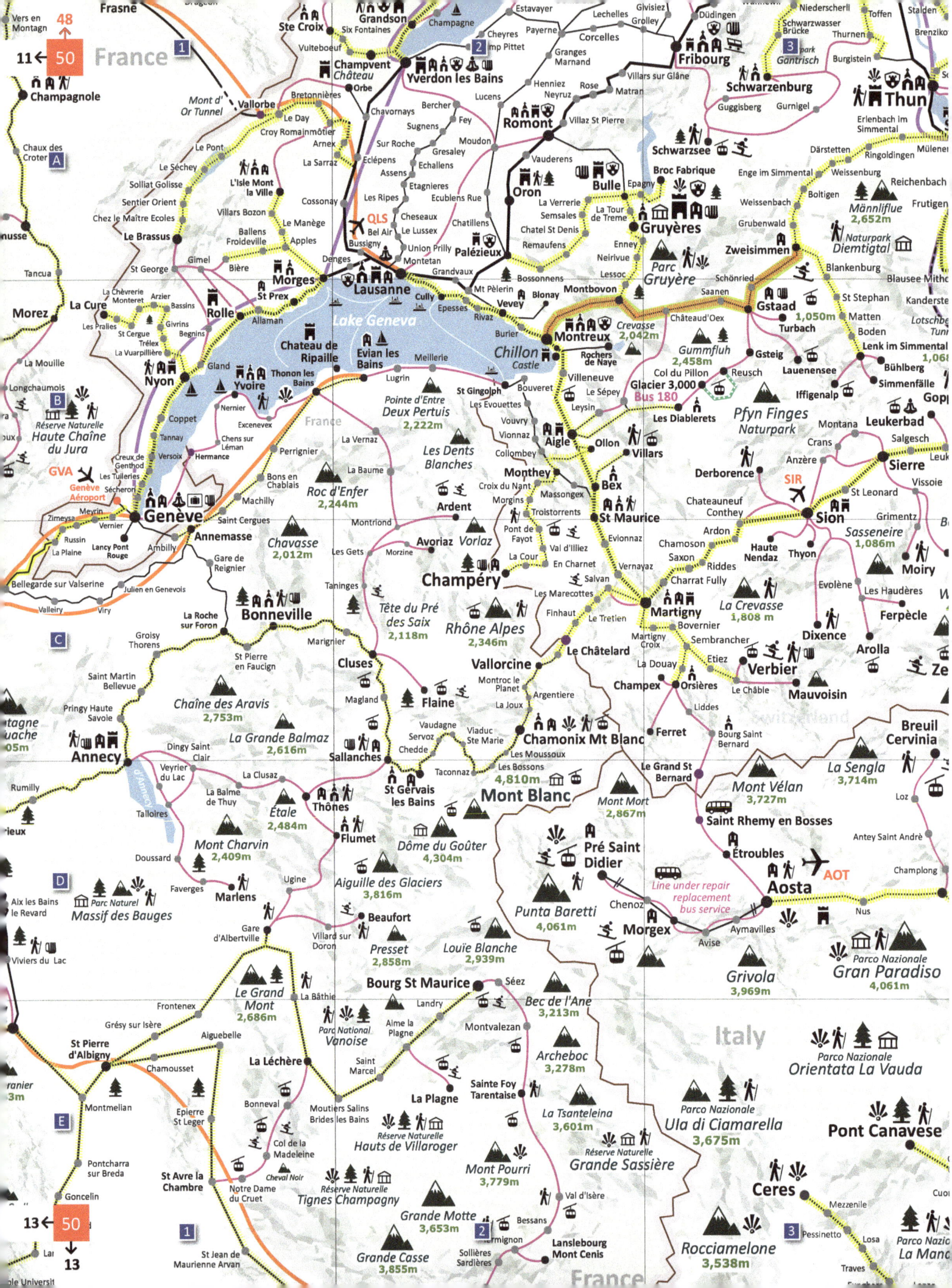

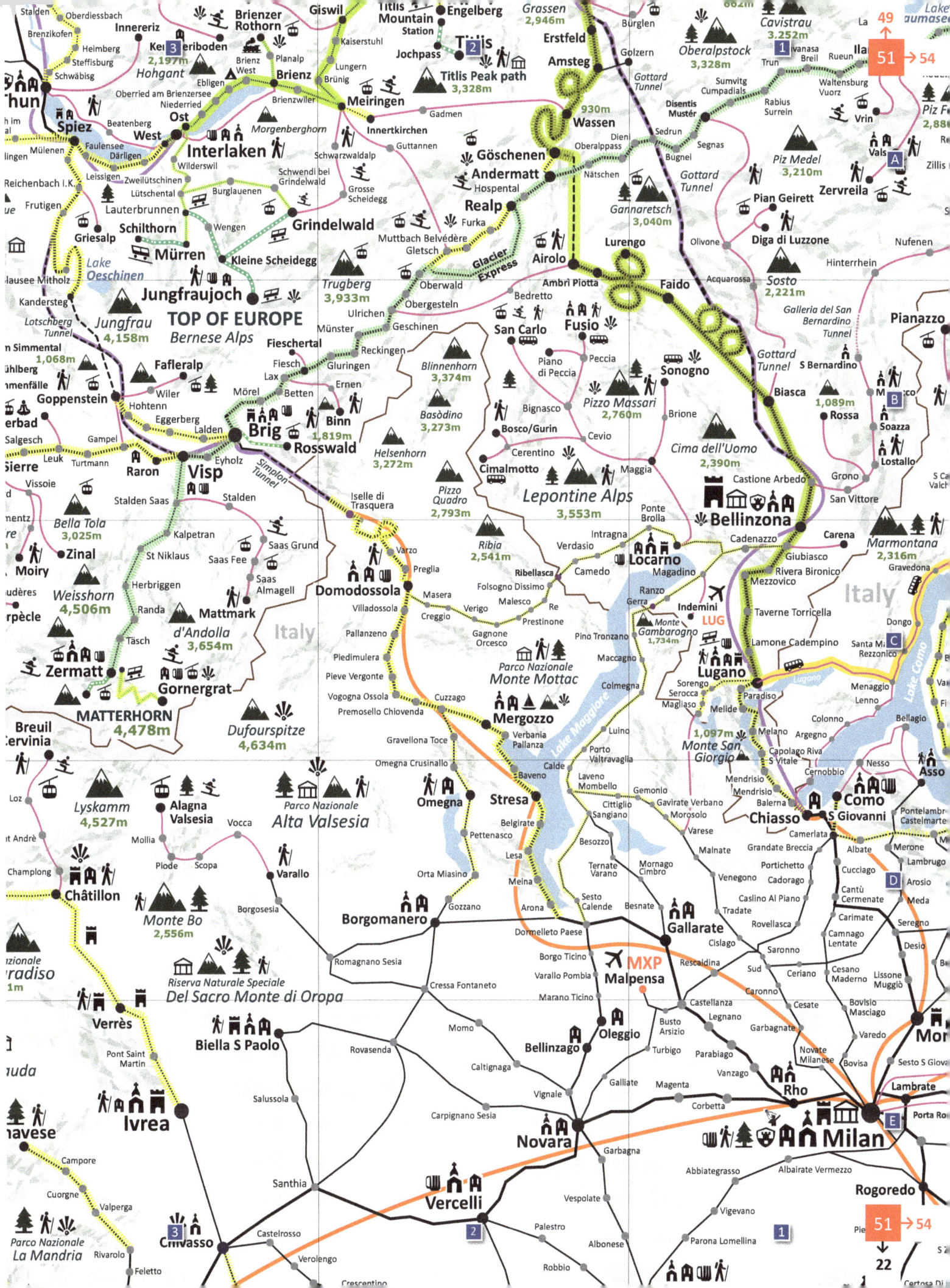

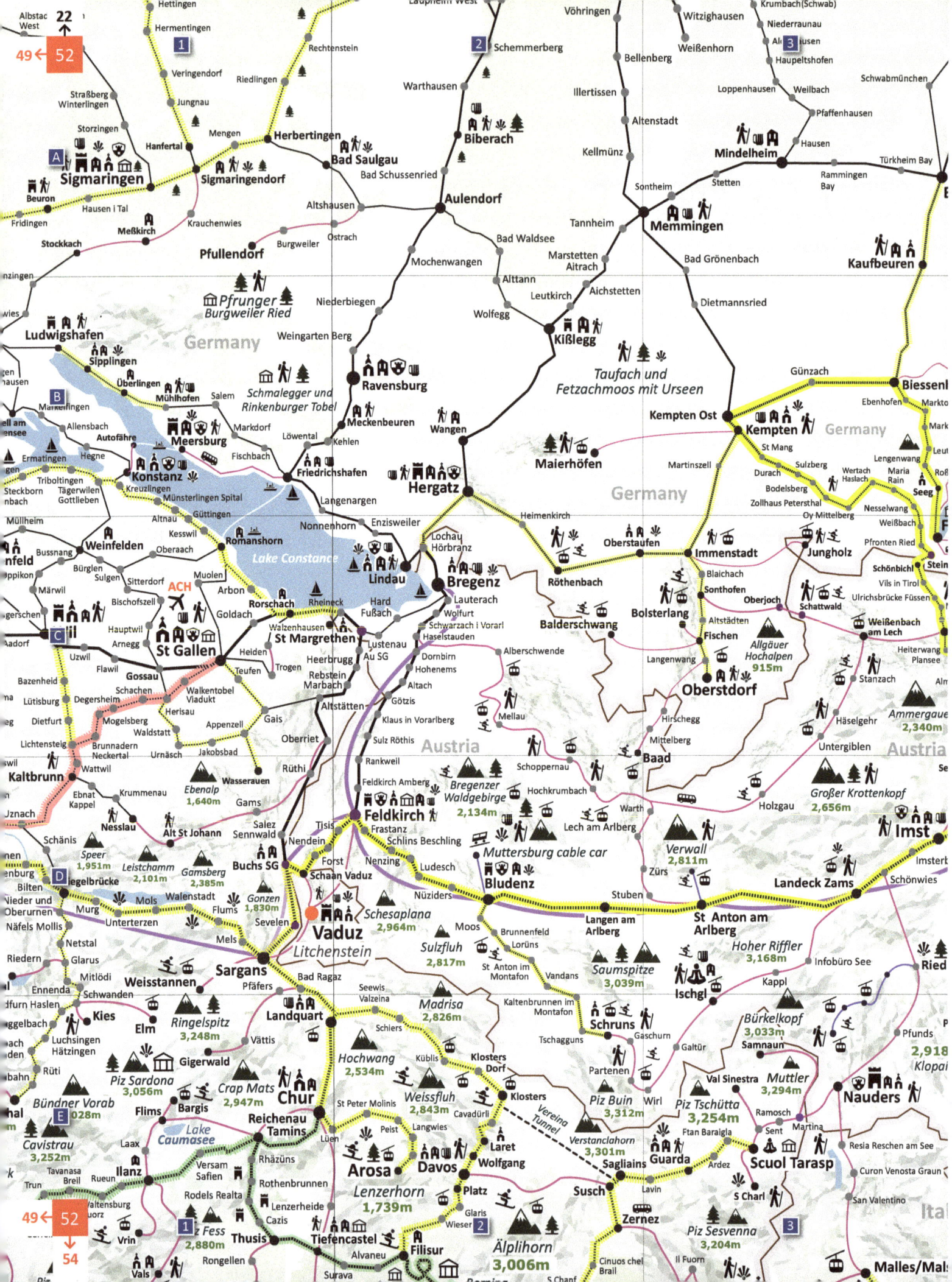

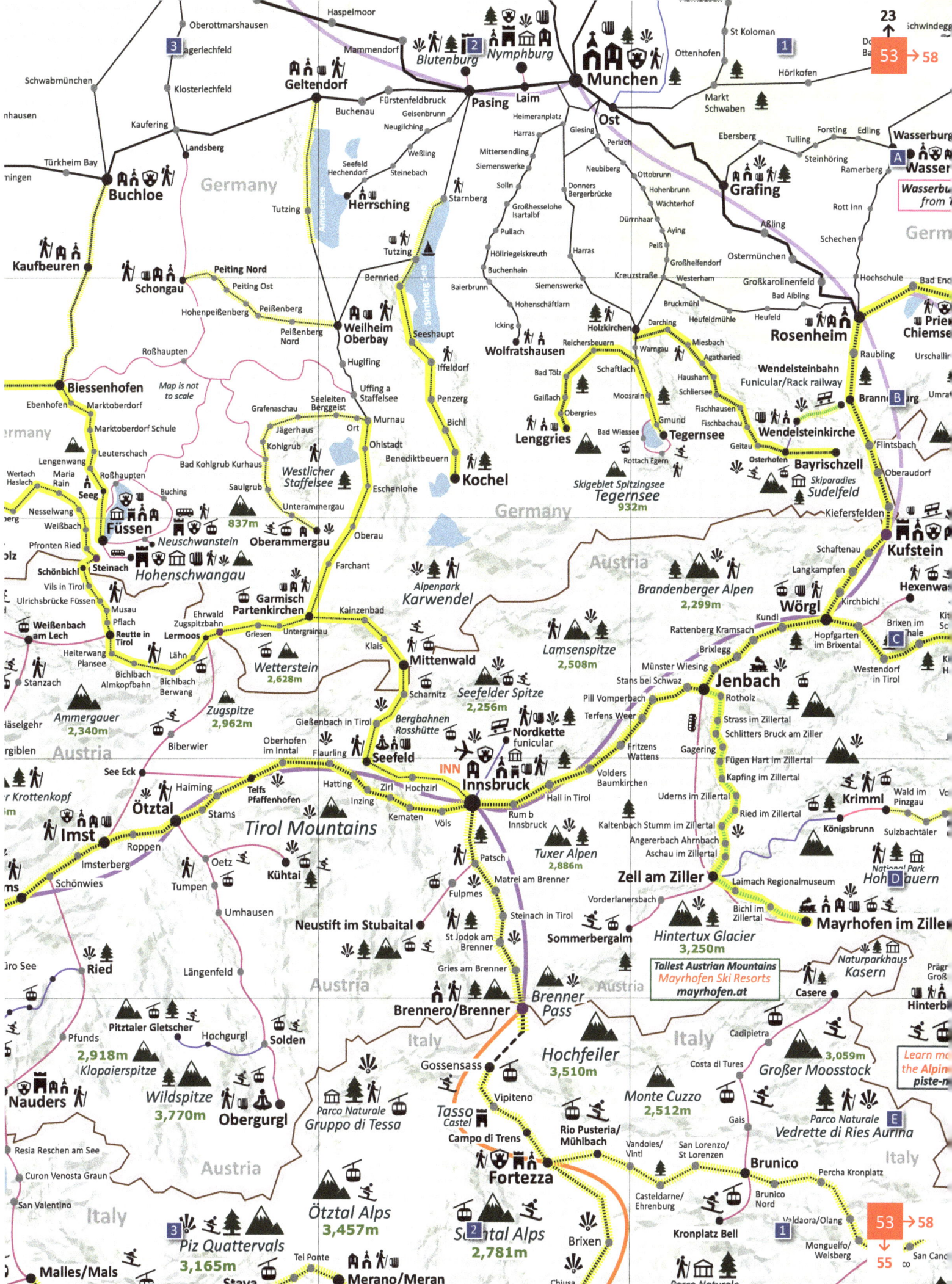

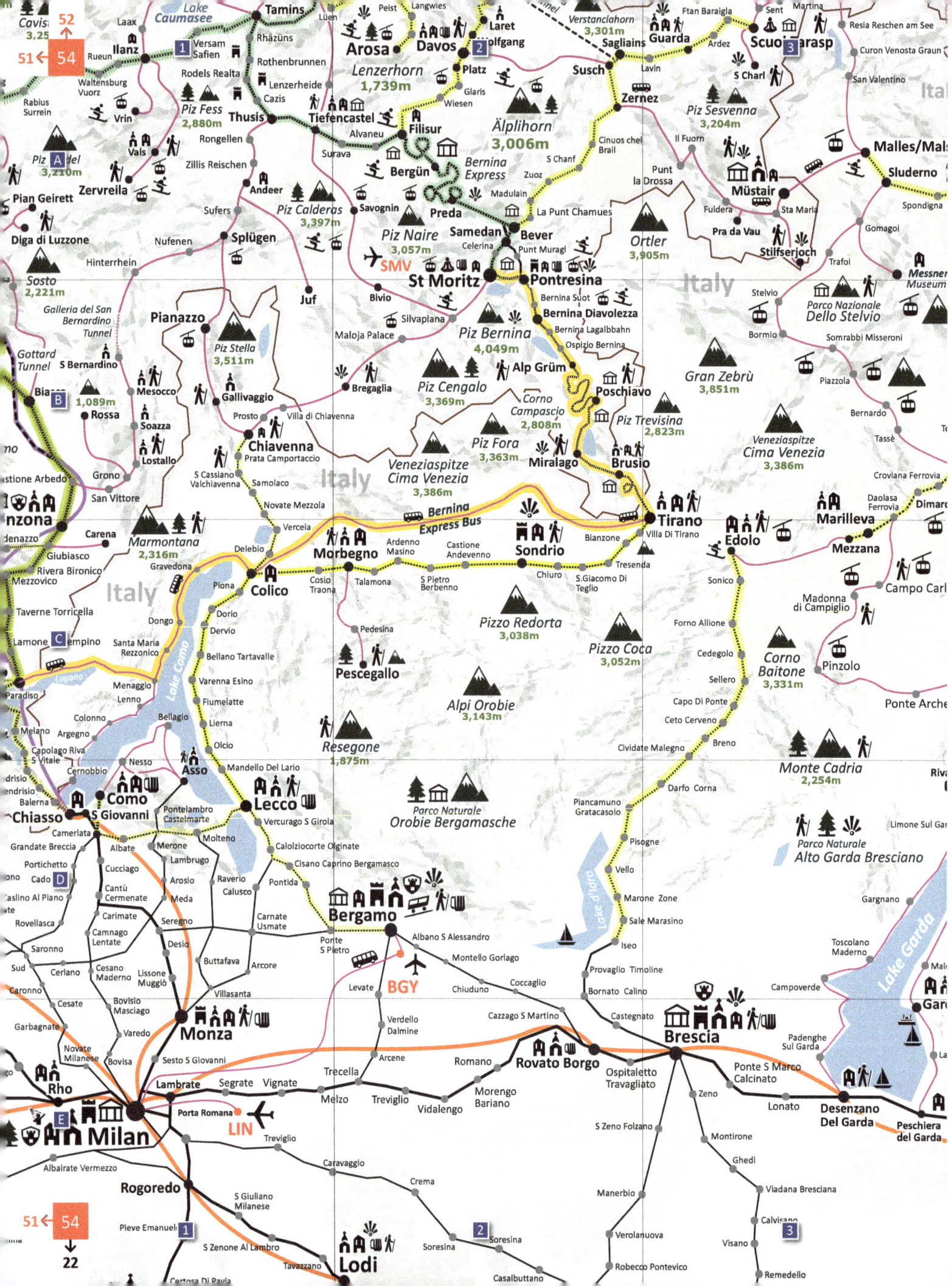

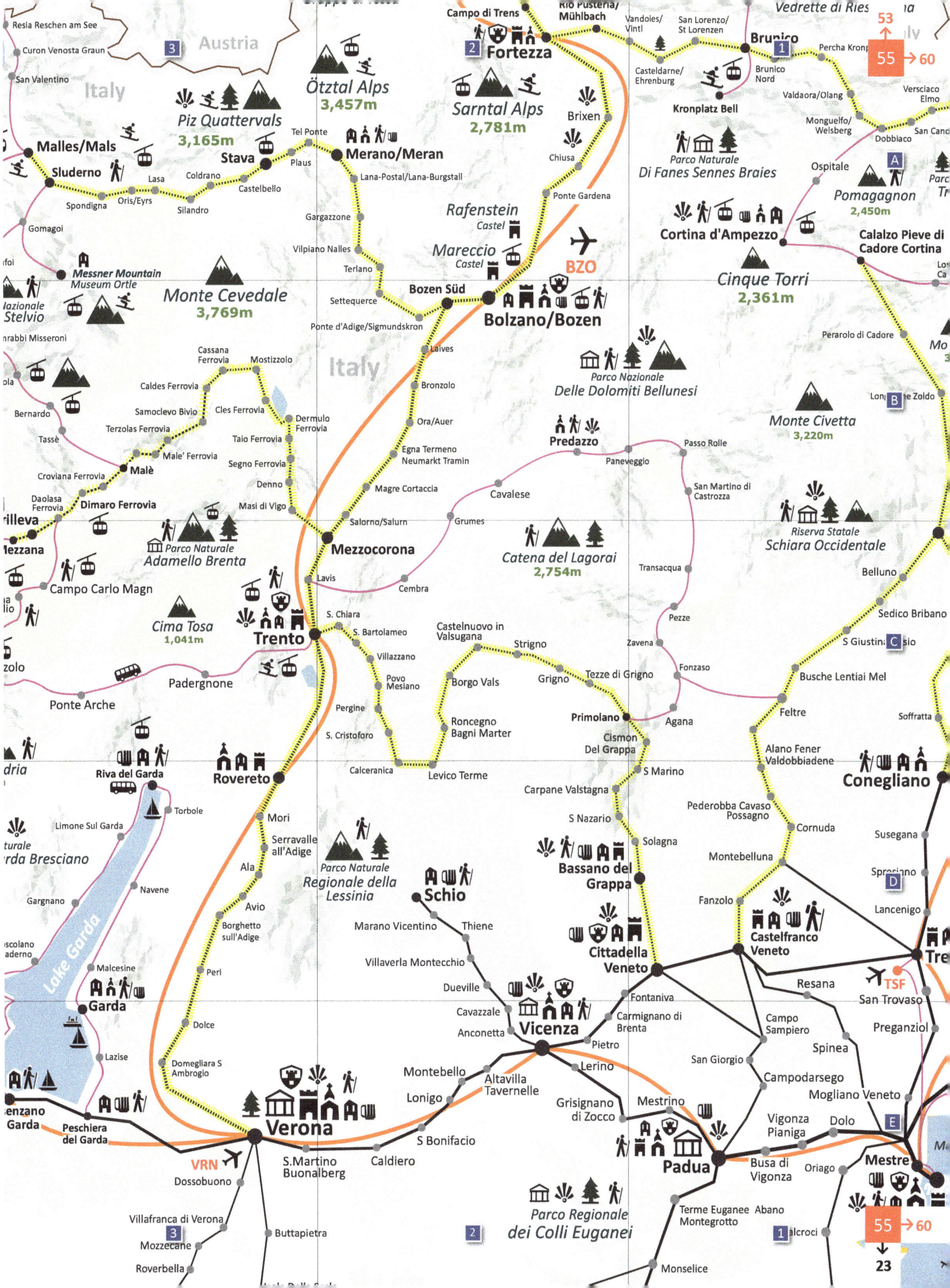

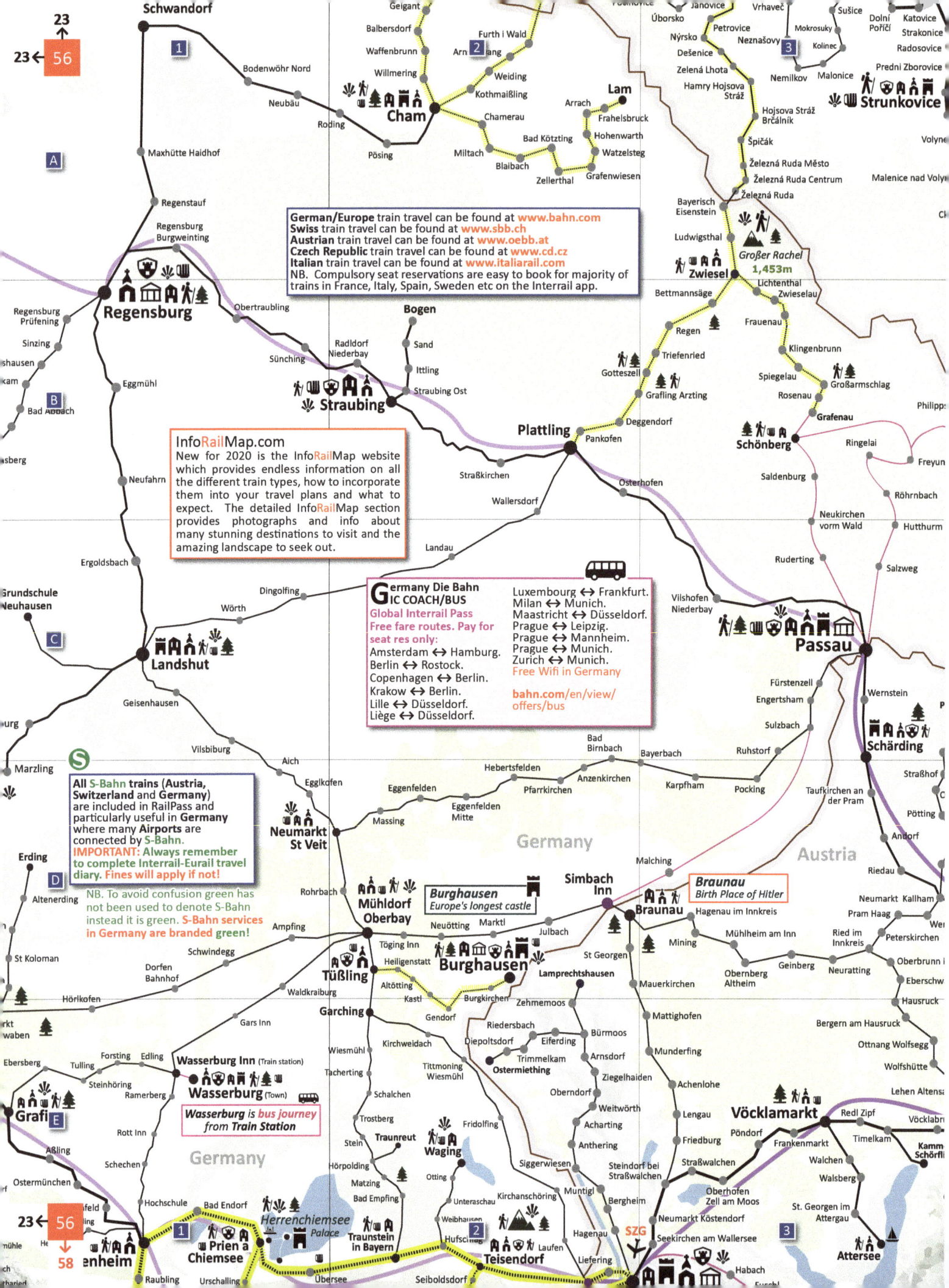

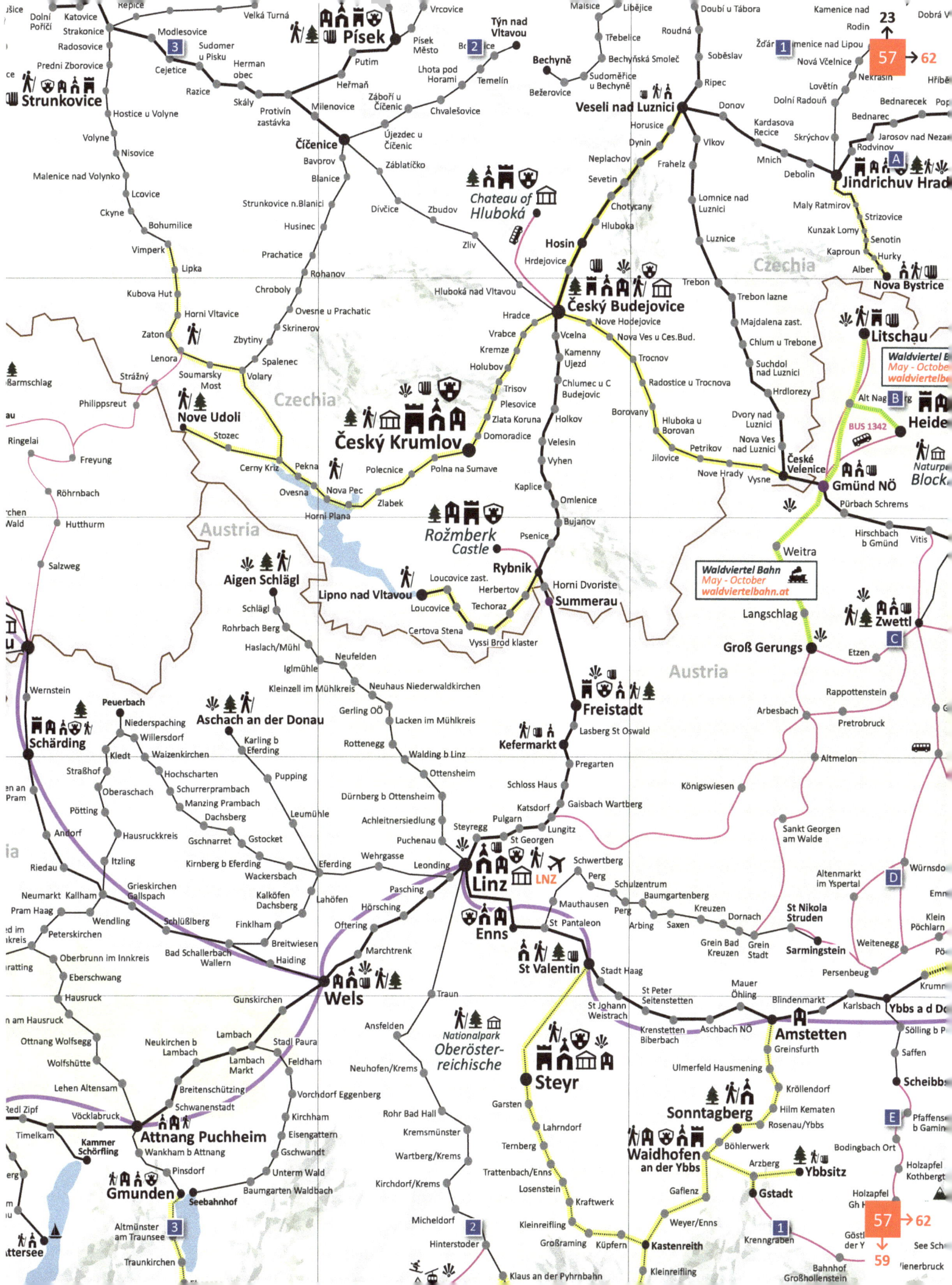

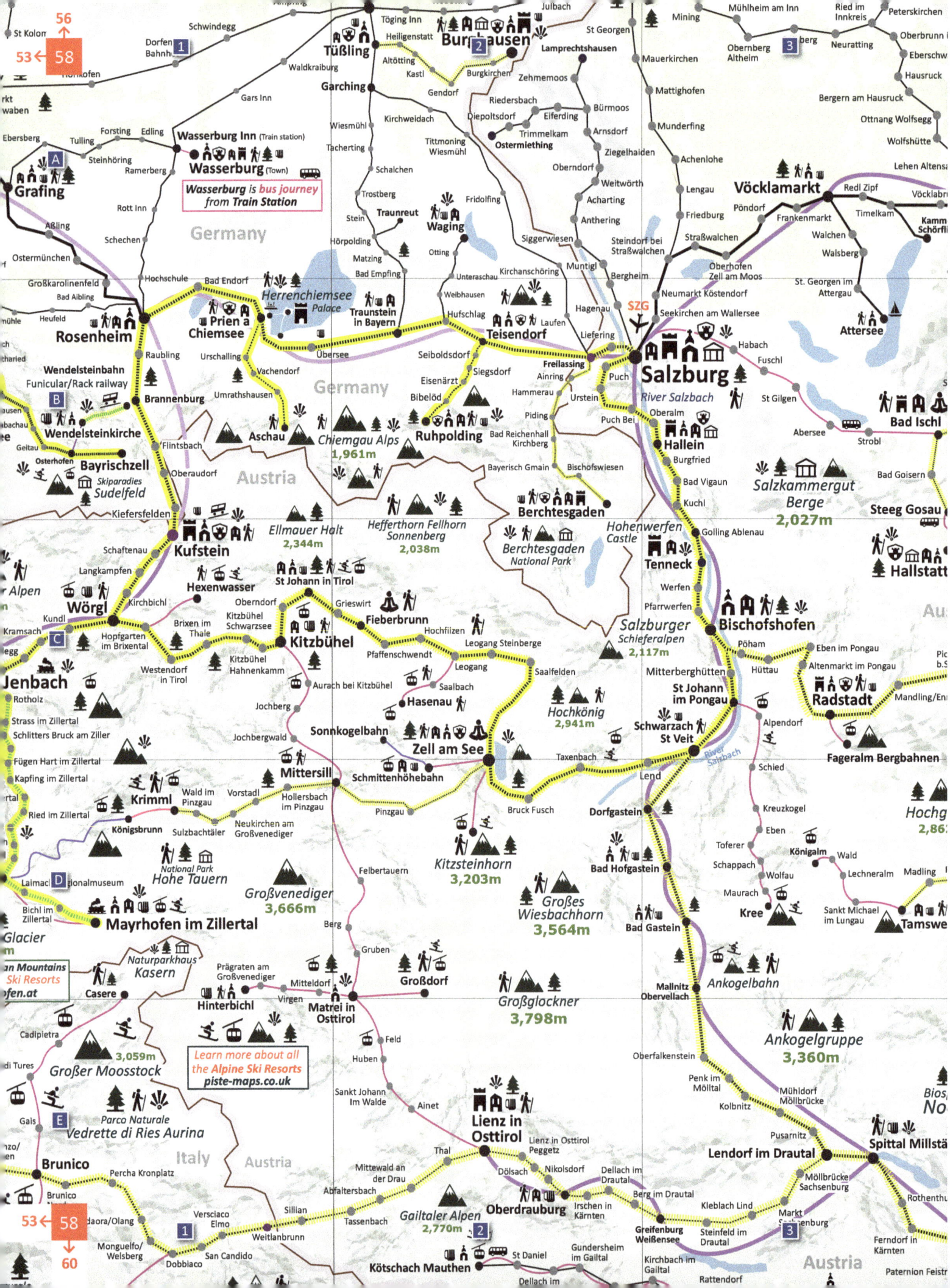

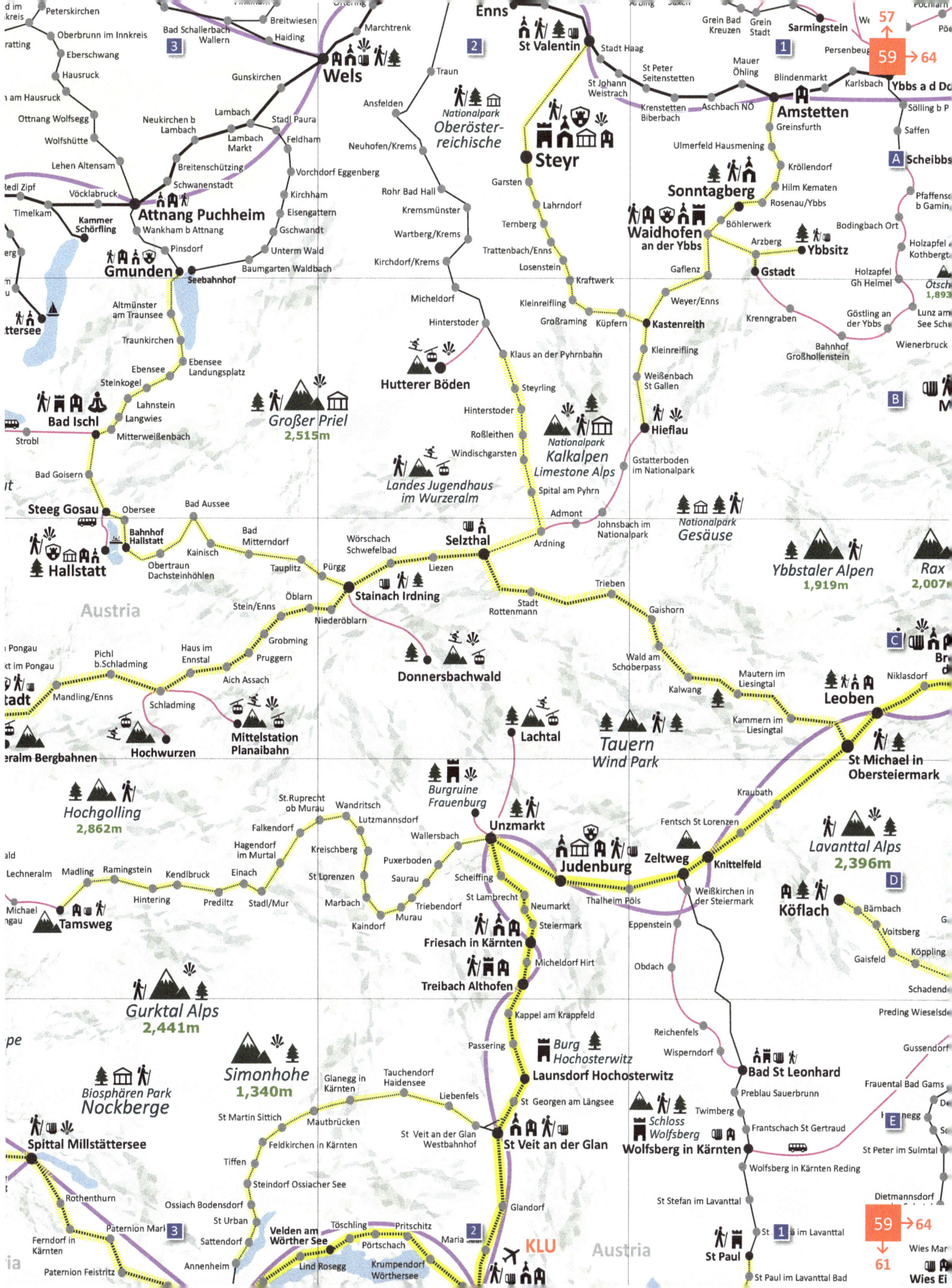

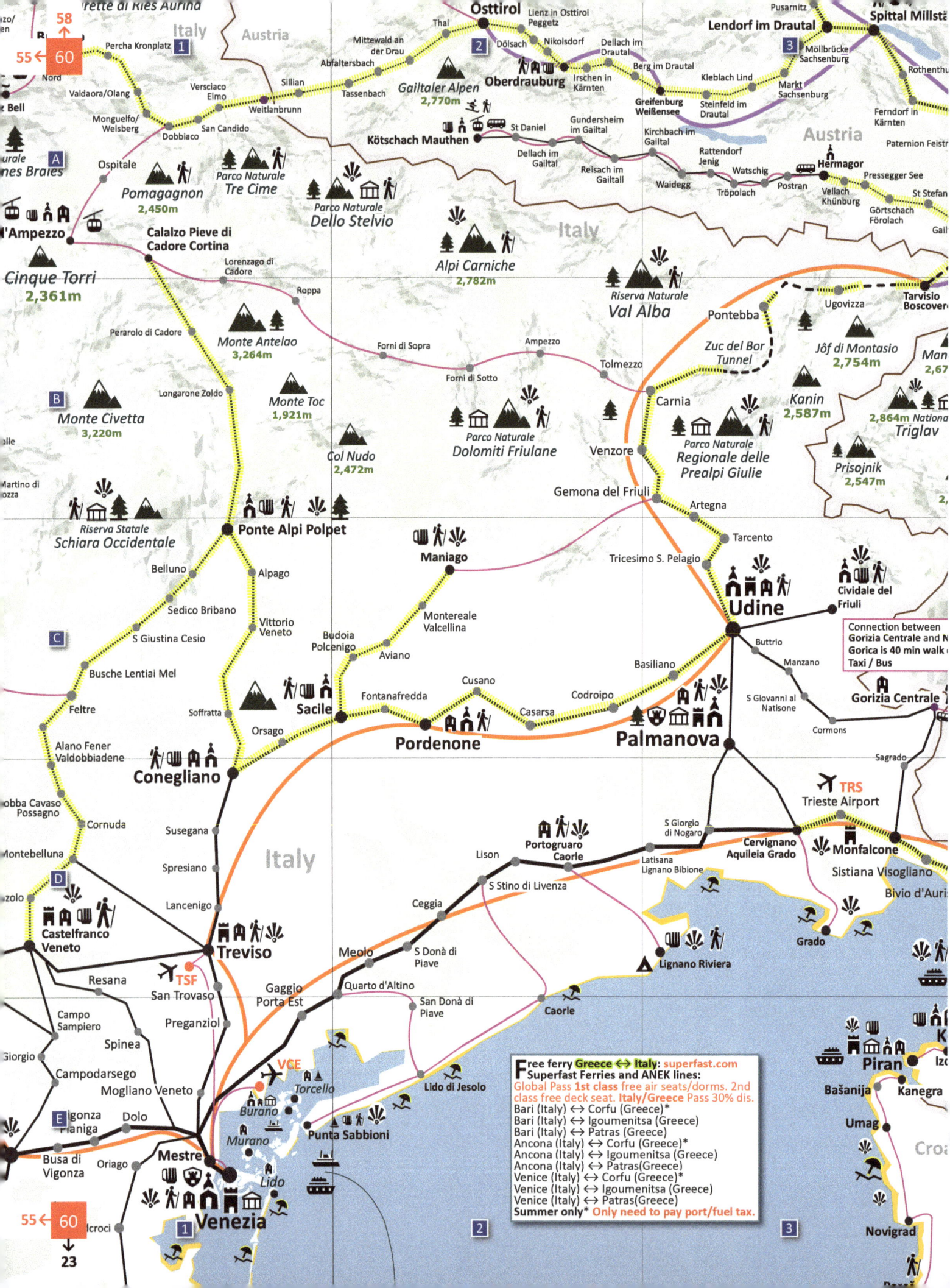

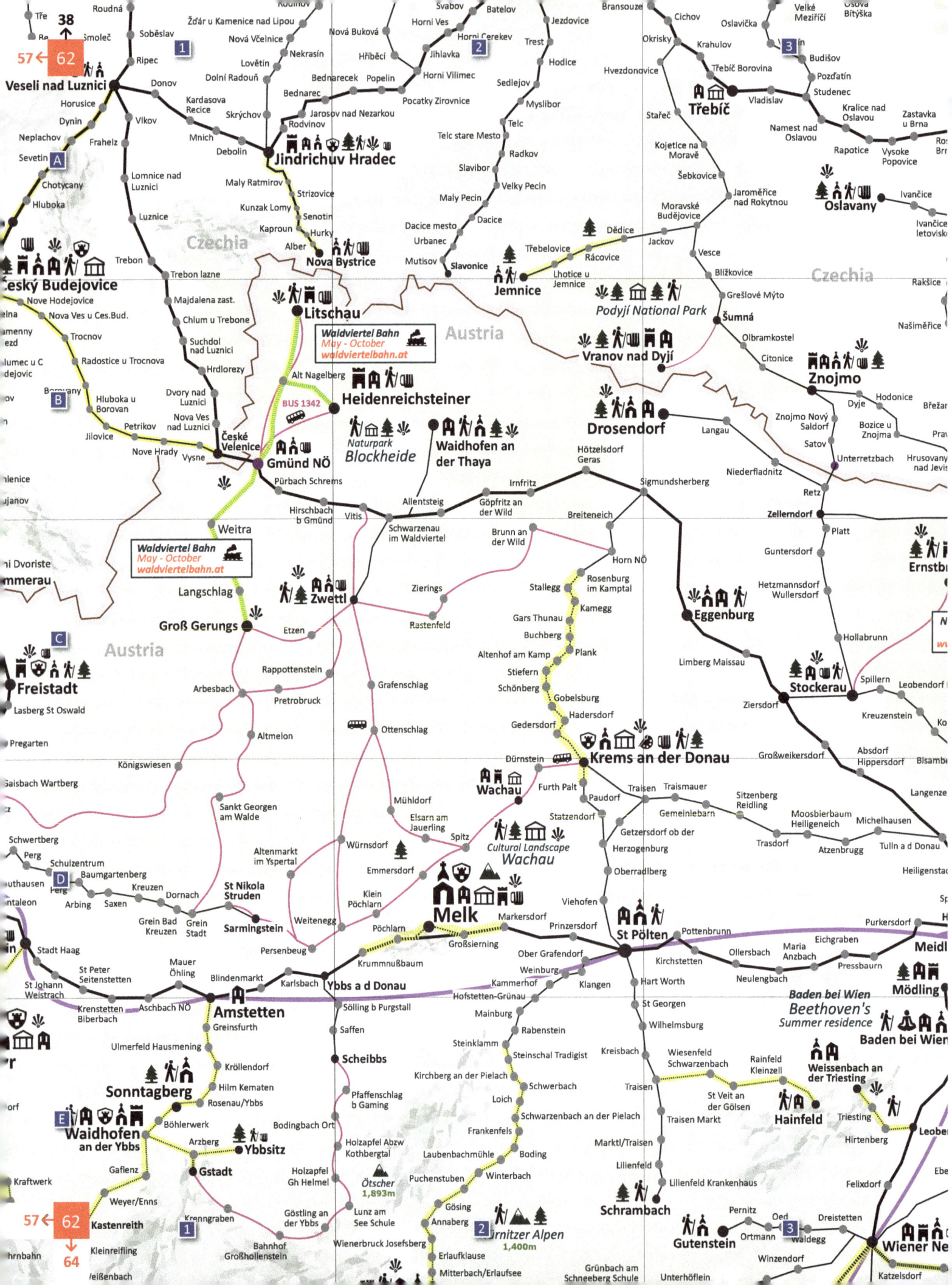

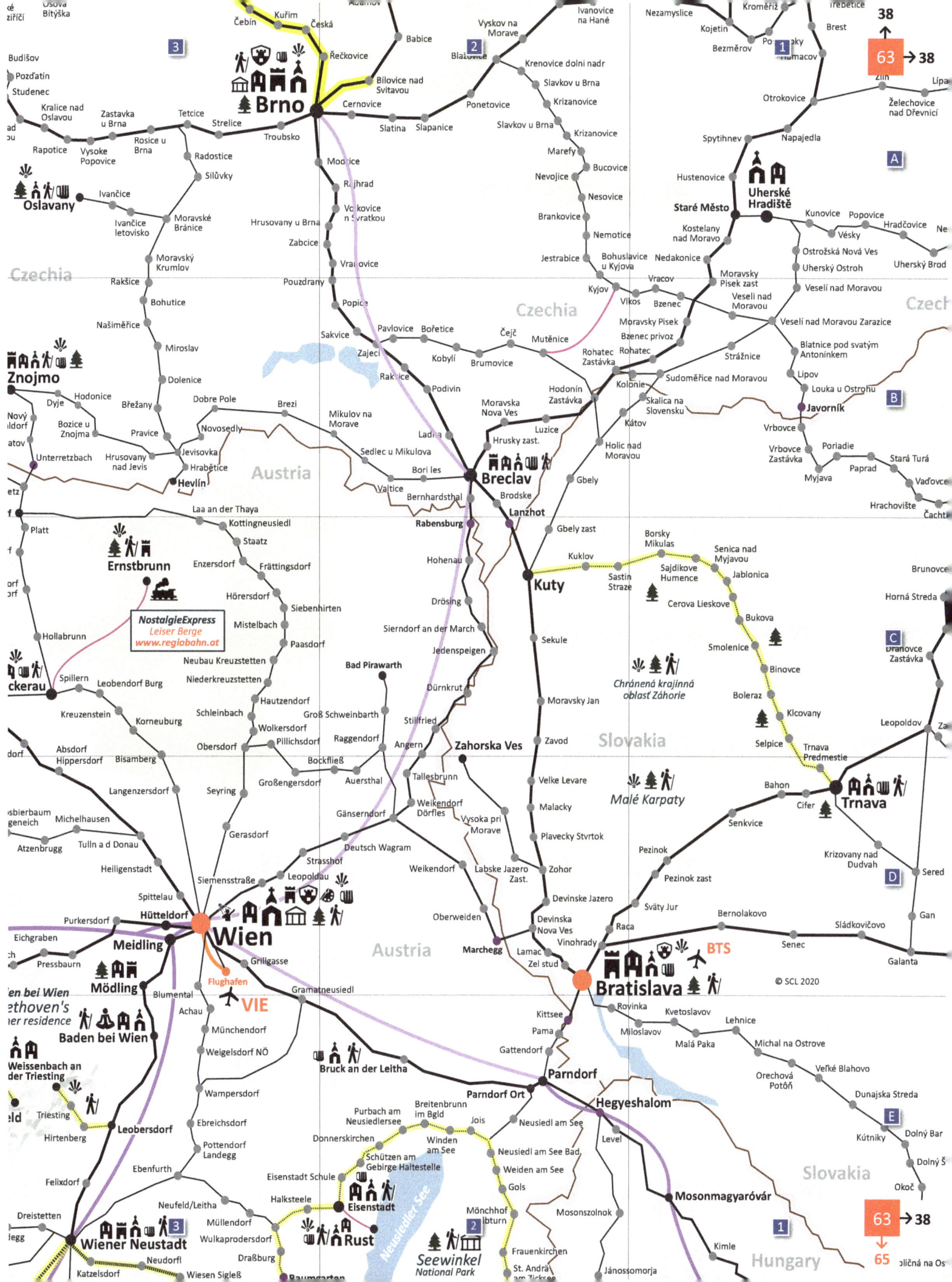

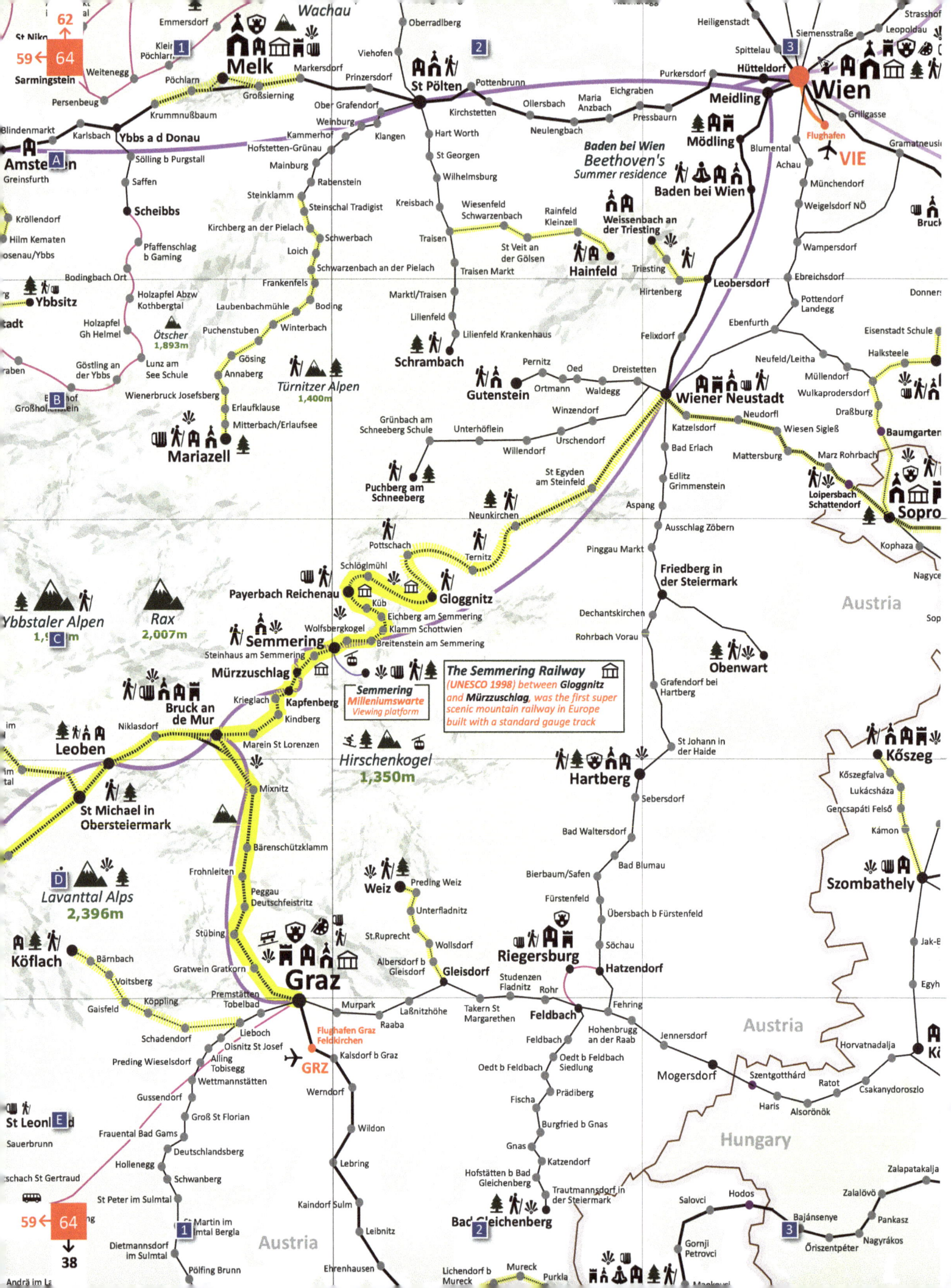

How to use the A-Z Index

Page numbers are displayed on both top and bottom left.

Arrows denote map navigation and are colour coded. **Black** arrows are basic Info**Rail**Map and Red arrows are detailed Info**Rail**Map pages.

Index entries are also colour coded with Capital cities in **bold red**, detailed Info**Rail**Map page numbers are in **red bold**.

Bilbao is located at grid reference **A1** on page **12**

Spain
..
Bilbao 1A 12
..

Index

A

Albania
Berat 3E 40
Durres 2A 27
Tirana 3D 40
Vlore 3E 40

Algeria
Algiers 3D 14
Annaba 2E 15
Bejaia 3D 15
Bizerte 2E 15
Blida 1E 19
Chlif 2E 19
Constantine 3E 15
Mostagenem 2E 19
Oran 2D 14
Skikda 3E 15

Andorra
Andorra 2B 12

Austria
Baden bei Wien 3A 64
Bad Ischl 3B 59
Bischofshofen 3C 58
Bludenz 2D 52
Bregenz 2C 52
Bruck an de Mur 1C 64
Feldkirch 2D 52
Freistadt 2C 57
Graz 1E 64
Graz 2C 38
Hallein 3B 58
Hallstatt 3C 59
Hartberg 2D 64
Imst 3D 53
Innsbruck 2D 53
Innsbruck 3C 23
Judenburg 2D 59
Krems an der Donau 2D 62
Kufstein 1C 58
Lienz in Osttirol 2E 58
Linz 2B 38
Linz 2D 57
Mayrhofen 1D 53
Melk 2B 38
Melk 2D 62
Muttenburg cable 2D 52
Radstadt 3C 58
Riegersburg 2D 64
Salzburg 2B 58
Salzburg 2C 23
Semmering 2C 64
Steyr 2B 38
Villach 3A 61
Wachau 2D 62
Wien 3B 38
Wien 3D 63
Zell am See 2D 58

B

Belgium
Aalst 1C 20
Antwerpen 1B 20
Arlon 2D 20
Brugge 1B 20
Brussels 1A 11
Charleroi 1C 20
Ghent 1C 20
Leuven 2C 20
Liege 2C 20
Lokeren 1C 20
Mechelen 1C 20
Mons 1C 20
Spa 2C 20
St Niklaas 1C 20
Tournai 1C 20
Turnhout 2B 20
Ypres 1C 20
Zeebrugge 1B 20

Bosnia
Doboj 2A 40
Mostar 3B 40
Sarajevo 3B 40
Travnik 2B 40

Bulgaria
Bansko 1D 41
Burgas 2A 45
Dobrinishte 1D 41
General Todorov 2D 41
Karlovo 1C 41
Koprivshtica 1C 41
Ovech Fortress 2A 45
Pleven 1B 41
Plovdiv 1C 41
Rila Monastery 2D 41
Ruse 3E 43
Sofija 1B 44
Svilengrad 3B 45
Varna 2A 45

C

Corsica (France)
Ajaccio 2C 24
Bastia 2B 24
Bonifacio 2C 24
L'ille Rousse 2B 24

Crete
Heraklion 3E 46
Kissamos 2E 46

Croatia
Dubrovnik 2C 40
Karlovac 2E 38
Kastel Stari 2B 40
Knin 2A 40
Ploce 2C 40
Pula 1E 38
Rijeka 2E 61
Rijeka (European Capital of Culture 2020) 2E 23
Sibenik 2B 40
Sisak 2E 38
Split 2B 40
Varazdin 2D 38
Viz 2B 40
Zadar 1A 40
Zagreb 2D 38

Cyprus
Ayia Napa 1E 47
Kyrenia 1E 47
Nicosia 1E 47

Czechia
Benesov 1E 21
Breclav 3B 38
Breznice 2A 23
Brno 3A 38
Castle Karlstejn 2E 21
Ceska Lipa 2D 36
Český Budejovice 2A 38
Český Budejovice 2B 57
Český Krumlov 2A 38
Český Krumlov 2B 57
Chateau Hlubaka 2A 57
Havlichav B. 1A 23
Horazdovice 2E 21
Hradec Kralove 1D 21
Jindrichuv Hradec 1A 62
Karlovy Vary 2D 21
Klatovy 2E 21
Liberec 2D 36
Olomouc 3E 36
Pardubice 3E 36
Plzen 2E 21
Praha 1E 21
Rakovnik 2D 36
Rozmberk Castle 2C 57
Strakonice 2A 38
Svihov 2E 21
Tabor 2E 36
Trebic 3A 38
Turnov 2D 36
Znojmo 3B 62

D

Denmark
Aalborg 2B 34
Aarhus 2C 34
Dragsholm 3C 34
Esbjerg 1C 34
Frederikshavn 2B 34
Grenaa 2C 34
Hillerod 3C 34
Hirtshals 2A 34
Kobenhavn 3C 34
Rodby 3D 34
Rosskilde 3C 34
Skagen 2A 34
Soenderborg 2D 34
Svendborg 2D 34
Tonder 2D 34
Vejle 2C 34

E

England (UK)
Bath Spa 3C 8
Berwick 2B 7
Birmingham 3A 9
Blackpool 3D 7
Bristol 3B 8
Cambridge 2B 9
Canterbury 2D 9
Carlisle 3B 7
Chester 3D 7
Dover 2D 9
Durham 2C 7
Ely 2B 9
Exeter 2C 8
Glastonbury 3C 8
Gloucester 3B 9
Guernsey 3E 9
Hastings 2D 9
Isle of Scilly 1D 8
Lancaster 3C 7
Leeds 2D 7
Lincoln 2E 7
Liverpool 3D 7
London 2C 9
Manchester 3D 7
Newcastle 2C 7
Newquay 1C 8
Norwich 1B 9
Nottingham 2A 9
Oxford 3B 9
Penzance 1C 8
Peterborough 2B 9
Plymouth 2C 8
Portsmouth 3D 9
Salisbury 3C 9
Shewsbury 3E 6
Southampton 3C 9
Stonehenge 3C 8
Stratford 3B 9
Weymouth 3D 8
Winchester 3C 9
Worcester 3B 8
York 2D 7

Estonia
Parnu 2D 31
Tallinn 2D 31
Tartu 2D 31

F

Finland
Helskinki 2C 31
Joensuu 1B 31
Kemijarvi 2C 29
Kolari 3C 29
Oulu 2A 31
Piekamaki 2B 31
Provoo 2C 31
Rovaniemi 2D 29
Seinajoki 3B 31
Tampere 3C 31
Turku Abo 3C 31

France
Agen 2A 12
Arcachon 2A 12
Argentan 3B 10
Arles 3C 13
Arras 2A 11
Auch 2A 12
Autun 2D 11
Auxerre 3C 11
Avignon 3C 13
Bayonne A2 12
Beauvais 3B 11

67

Belfort 1D 11
Bethune 2A 11
Bordeaux 2E 10
Bourges 3D 11
Briancon 2B 13
Brive 3E 10
Caen 3A 10
Cahors 3A 12
Calais 1D 9
Cambrai 2A 11
Cannes 2C 13
Carcassonne 3B 12
Cerbere 3C 12
Chalon sur Saone 2D 11
Chamouix Mont Blanc 2C 50
Chartes 3B 11
Chateau Gontier 3C 10
Chateauroux 3D 10
Chaumont 2C 11
Cherbourg 3A 10
Chinon 3C 10
Cognac 2D 10
Condom 2A 12
Dieppe 1E 9
Dijon 2D 11
Dole 2D 11
Douai 2A 11
Dreux 3B 10
Evreux 3B 11
Flers 3B 10
Forbach 2D 20
Gaillac 3A 12
Gourdon 3A 12
Grenoble 2B 13
Guingamp 2B 10
Hyeres 2D 13
Lamballe 2B 10
Lannion 1A 10
La Rochelle 2D 10
La Tour De Carol 3C 12
Le Mans 3C 10
Le Monastier 3A 13
Le Puye 3A 13
Lille 2A 11
Loches 3C 10
Lourdes 2A 12
Luchon 2B 12
Lyon 3E 11
Macon 2E 11
Marseille 3D 13
Marvejols 3A 13
Metz 1C 11
Mezin 2E 10
Montaugan Ville Bourbon 3A 12
Montbard 2D 11
Monte Carlo 1C 13
Montelimar 3B 13
Morlaix 1A 10
Moulins sur Allier 3D 11
Mulhouse 2B 22
Nancy 1C 11
Nantes 2C 10
Narbonne 3C 12
Neufchateau 1C 11
Nevers 3D 11
Nice 1A 24
Nimes 3C 13
Niort 2D 10
Orange 3B 13
Orleans 3C 11
Orthez 2A 12
Paimpol 2A 10
Paris 3B 11
Perigueux 3E 10
Pointers 3D 10
Quimper 1B 10
Quimperle 1B 10
Redon 2B 10
Reims 2B 11
Rennes 2B 10
Rodez 3A 12
Roscoff 1A 10
Rouen 3B 11
Sable 3C 10
Sadan 2D 20
Sarlat la Caneda 3A 12
Selestat 1D 11
Sens 2C 11
Severac le Chateau 3A 12
St Amand 2A 11
St Ambroix 3B 13
St Brieuc 2B 10
St Dizier 2C 11
St Jean Pied 2A 12
St Maixent 3D 10
St Malo 2B 10
St Quentin 2B 11
Strasbourg 2A 22
St Tropez 2D 13
Tarbes 2B 12
Tonnerre 2C 11
Toulon 2D 13
Toulouse 2B 12
Tours 3C 10
Troyes 2C 11
Uzerche 3E 10
Valance 3B 13
Valenciennes 2A 11
Vannes 2B 10
Versailles 3B 11
Vezene Valley 3E 10
Vierzon 3C 11

G

Germany
Aachen 2C 20
Alsfeld 3C 21
Altomunster 3B 23
Ansbach 3E 21
Augsburg 3B 23
Bacharach 3D 20
Bamberg 3D 21
Bayreuth 3D 21
Bayrischzell 1B 58
Berchtesgarden 1C 38
Berlin 2B 21
Bielefeld 3B 20
Blutenburg 3B 23
Bonn 3C 20
Brandenburg 2C 21
Braunfels Castle 3C 20
Bremen 3B 20
Buchloe 3B 23
Burg Eltz 3D 20
Burghausen 2D 56
Celle 3B 21
Cochem Castle 3D 20
Dessau 2C 21
Doberlug 2C 21
Dortmund 3B 20
Dresden 2C 36
Duisburg 3B 20
Eichstatt 3A 23
Erfurt 3C 21
Flensburg 2D 34
Fluda 3C 21
Frankfurt 3D 20
Furth 3E 21
Fussen 3C 53
Gottingen 3C 21
Hahenzottern Castle 3A 22
Hamburg 2E 34
Hanau 3D 20
Hannover 3B 21
Hanstein Castle 3C 21
Heibronn 3E 20
Hergatz 3B 22
Herrenberg 3E 20
Horb 3A 22
Ingolstadt 3E 21
Kaiserslautem 3D 20
Karlsruhe 3E 20
Kassel 3C 21
Koblenz 3C 20
Koln 3C 20
Konstanz 2A 49
Landshut 1C 56
Leipzig 2C 21
Limburg 3C 20
Lindau 3B 22
Lubeck 2E 34
Ludwigslust 1B 36
Luneburg 3B 21
Mains 3D 20
Mannheim 3D 20
Marburg 3C 20
Meersburg 1B 52
Mittenwald 2C 53
Moritzburg Castle 2C 21
Munchen 2A 53
Munchen 3B 23
Munchen Parsing 3B 23
Munster 3B 20
Norden 3A 20
Nurnberg 3E 21
Nymphenburg 3B 23
Osnabruck 3B 20
Parsburg 3E 21
Passau 2B 38
Passau 3C 56
Plochingen 3E 20
Potsdam 2C 21
Puttgarden 3D 34
Regensburg 3A 23
Rosenheim 1B 58
Rostock 2A 21
Rotenburg 3C 21
Rudolstadt 3C 21
Saaburg 2D 20
Sasanitz 1A 21
Sigmaringen 3B 22
Singen 2A 49
Straubing 2B 56
Straubling 2A 23
Stuttgart 3E 20
Tegernsee 1B 53
Trier 2D 20
Tubingen 3A 22
Ulm 3A 22
Waldenburg 3E 20
Warburg 3C 21
Wasserburg 1E 56
Wisenburg 2C 21
Wittenberg 2C 21
Worms 3D 20
Wurzburg 3D 21

Greece
Aegina 2C 46
Alexandropolis 3C 45
Athens 2C 46
Corfu 2C 27
Delphi 2B 46
Florina 3E 41
Halikidhiki Beaches 2D 44
Kalamata 1C 46
Kalambaka 1A 46
Korinthos 2C 46
Methoni 1D 46
Monemvasia 2D 46
Mystras 2D 46
Nafplion 2C 46
Naxos 3C 47
Olympia 1C 46
Patras 1B 46
Pylos 1D 46
Rhodos 2D 47
Santorini 3D 47
Sigri 3E 45
Sparta 2C 46
Thessaloniki 1D 44
Volos 1E 44
Zakinthos 1C 46

H

Hungary
Budapest 3C 39
Cegled 2C 39
Debrecen 2C 39
Eger 2B 39
Esztergom 3B 39
Gyor 3C 38
Kecskemet 3C 39
Koszeg 3C 38
Miskolc 2B 39
Nyiregyhaza 2C 39
Papa 3C 38
Pecs 3E 38
Siofok 3D 39
Sopron 3B 65
Sopron 3C 38
Szeged 3E 39

I

Ireland (Republic)
Athlone 2C 3
Ballina 3B 3
Birr Castle 2D 3
Blarney Stone 2E 3
Bray 1D 3
Cork 2E 3
Donegal 2B 3
Dublin 1C 3
Ennis 2D 3
Galway 2C 3
Howth 1C 3
Limerick 2D 3
Listowel 3D 3
Moneghan 1B 3
Rosslare 1D 3
The Currach 1D 3
Tralee 3D 3
Trim Castle 2C 3
Waterford 1D 3
Westport 3C 3

Ireland (UK)
Antrim 1B 3
Belfast 1B 3
Carrickfergus 1B 3
Downpatrick 1B 3
Enniskillen 2B 3
Giants Causeway 1A 3
Larne Harbour 1B 3
Londonderry 2A 3
Winterfell Castle 1B 3

Isle of Man (UK)
Castletown 3C 6
Douglas 3B 6
Ramsey 3B 6

Italy
Acqui Terme 2E 22
Agropoli Castellabate 3E 25
Alessandria 2D 22
Ancona 3B 25
Arezzo 3B 24
Assisi 3B 25
Bari 2E 25
Barletta 3A 27
Battipaglia 3E 25
Benevento 3D 25
Bergamo 2D 54
Bergamo 3D 22
Bernalda 2E 25
Bologna 3A 24
Bolzano 2B 55
Bolzano 3D 22
Brescia 3E 54
Brindisi 2B 27
Capri 3E 25
Carpinone 3D 25
Caserta 3D 25
Cassino 3D 25
Castle di Sangro 3D 25
Chiasso 1D 51
Civitavecchia 3C 24
Colico 1C 54
Como 1D 54

Consenza 3C 27
Cortina 1A 55
Domodossola 2C 51
Ferrara 3A 24
Firenze 3B 24
Foggia 2D 25
Fortezza 2E 55
Fortezza Aragonese 3C 27
Fossano 2D 22
Gallipoli 2C 27
Genova 2A 24
Groseto 3C 24
Ivrea 2D 22
Lamenzia 3C 27
Lanciano 3C 25
L'Aquila 3C 25
La Spezia 2A 24
Lecco 1D 54
Leece 2B 27
Lodi 3D 22
Loreto 3B 25
Lucca 3B 24
Lucera 2D 25
Lugo 3A 24
Malpensa 1D 51
Manfredonia 2D 25
Massa 2A 24
Matera 3B 27
Melfi 2E 25
Merano 2A 55
Metaponto 3B 27
Milan 2D 22
Montepuiciano 3B 24
Monza 1E 54
Mortara 2D 22
Napoli 3D 25
Novara 2E 51
Orvieto 3B 24
Otranto 2C 27
Padua 3D 22
Palmanova 3D 23
Palmonova 3C 60
Pavia 2D 22
Pergola 3B 25
Pescara 3C 25
Peschici 2D 25
Piombino 2B 24
Pisa 2B 24
Pistoia 3B 24
Pompei 3E 25
Potenza 3B 27
Prato 3B 24
Reggio 3D 26
Rimini 3B 25
Roma 3C 24
Roveroto 3D 55
Rovigo 3E 22
Salerno 3E 25
Saluzzo 1D 22
San Marino 3B 24
Sansepolcro 3B 25
Sapri 3B 26
Sarzana 2A 24
Savona 1C 13
Sicignano 3E 25
Siena 3B 24
Sondrio 2C 54

Sorrento 3E 25
Spoleto 3C 25
Taranto 3B 27
Teramo 3C 25
Termoli 2C 25
Terracina 3D 24
Tirano 3C 54
Tivoli 3C 24
Torino 2D 22
Trento 3C 55
Treviso 1D 60
Trieste 3E 23
Tropea 3C 26
Udine 3C 60
Venice 3E 23
Verona 3D 22
Verona 3E 55
Vercelli 2D 22
Vicenza 2E 55
Vieste 2D 25
Viterbo 3C 24

K
Kosovo
Preshtine 3C 41

L
Latvia
Liepaga 1A 66
Riga 2A 66
Sigulda 3A 66
Ventspils 1A 66
Liechtenstein
Vaduz 1C 49
Lithuania
Curonian Spit 1B 66
Daugavpils 3B 66
Kaunas 2C 66
Klaipeda 1B 66
Siaullai 2B 66
Trakai 2C 66
Vilnius 3C 66
Luxembourg
Luxembourg 2D 20

M
Macedonia
Lake Ohrid 3E 41
Skopje 3D 41
Vales 3D 41
Malta
Vallatta 2E 26
Montenegro
Bar Port 3C 40
Podjorica 3C 40
Morocco
Casablanca 1E 18
Fes 2E 18
Meknes Amir 2E 18
Melilla 3E 18
Oujda 3E 18
Rabat 1E 18
Tanger 2D 18
Telouan 2D 18

N
Netherlands
Alkmaar 1A 20
Amersfoort 2B 20
Amsterdam 2B 20
Breda 2B 20
Den Haag 1B 20
Den Helder 2A 20
Deventer 2B 20
Eindoven 2B 20
Gouda 1B 20
Groningen 2A 20
Hook 1B 20
Hoorn 2A 20
Leeuwarden 2A 20
Leiden 1B 20
Maastricht 2C 20
Nijmegen 2B 20
Rotterdam 1B 20
S-Hertogenbosch 2B 20
Tilburg 2B 20
Utrecht 2B 20
Valkenburg 2C 20
Venlo 2B 20
Vlissingen 1B 20
Willemstad Castle 1B 20
Zutphen 2B 20
Zwolle 2B 20
Norway
Bergen 1D 32
Bodo 1C 28
Flam 2D 32
Hammerfest 3A 29
Kirkenes 1B 29
Kristiansand 2E 32
Lillehammer 2C 32
Mosjoeen 1D 28
Narvik 2C 28
Oslo 3D 32
Preikostolen 1D 32
Roros 3C 32
Stavanger 1E 32
Tromso 3B 28
Trondheim 2B 32
Vadso 1A 29
Vardo 1A 29

P
Poland
Augustow 2C 66
Auschwitz 3E 37
Biala Podlaska 1C 37
Blalogard 3A 36
Braniewo 1D 35
Bydgoszcz 2E 35
Ciechanow 2B 37
Czestochowa 3D 37
Darlowo 3A 36
Elk 2C 66
Gdansk 2D 35
Gdynia 2D 35
Gora Kalwaria 2C 37
Jelenia Gora 2D 36
Katowice 3D 37
Kielce 2D 37
Kolobrzeg 2A 36
Krakow 2E 37
Krynica 2A 39
Krzyz 3B 36
Krzyztopor Castle 2D 37
Kwidzyn 3A 37
Leba 3A 37
Lodz 3C 37
Lowics 2C 37
Lubin 2D 37
Malbork 3A 37
Niedzica Castle 2A 39
Olsztyn Glowny 1E 35
Ometa 1E 35
Opole 3D 37
Paczkow 3D 36
Poznan 3C 36
Przemys 1E 37
Raciborz 3D 37
Rzeszow 2E 37
Skierniewice 2C 37
Slupsk 3A 36
Stargard 2B 36
Swinoujscie 1A 21
Szczecin 2B 36
Torun 3B 37
Warsaw 2C 37
Wisnicz Castle 2E 37
Wroclaw 3D 36
Zakopane 2A 39
Zamosc 1D 37
Portugal
Beja 1B 18
Belver 2D 16
Braga 2C 16
Cacem 1B 18
Castle Batalha 1D 16
Castle Mavao 2E 16
Coimbra 1D 16
Evora 2B 18
Faro 1C 18
Lagos 1C 18
Leiria 1D 16
Lisboa 1A 18
Obidos 1A 18
Pocinho 3C 16
Pombal 1D 16
Porto 2C 16
Porto de Sines 1B 18
Sesimbra 1B 18
Setabal 1B 18
Sintra 1A 18
Tavira 1C 18
Viana do Castelo 2B 16

R
Romania
Adjud 2C 43
Arad 1C 42
Bacau 2B 43
Baia Mare 2A 42
Beclean 3B 42
Brasov 3C 43
Bucursti 3D 43
Caransebes 1D 42
Cluj Napoca 2B 42
Comamic 3C 43
Constanta 1D 43
Craiova 2E 42
Dej Calatori 3B 42
Iasi 2A 43
Mangalia 1D 43
Oradea 2B 42
Podu Olt 1A 41
Satu Mare 2A 42
Sibiu 3C 42
Sighisoara 3C 42
Sinaia 3C 43
Suceava 2A 43
Timisoara 3E 39
Vatra Dornei 3A 43

Russia
Kaliningrad 1C 66
St Petersburg 1C 31

S
Sardinia (Italy)
Alghero 1D 24
Cagliari 2E 24
Olbia 2D 24
Scotland (UK)
Aviemore 2C 5
Aye 3A 6
Ben Nevis 3C 5
Blair Castle 3D 5
Dingwall 3B 5
Dumfries 3B 7
Edinburgh 3E 5
Eilean Donan Castle 3C 5
Fort William 3C 5
Glasgow 3E 5
Inverness 3C 5
Islay 2D 4
Kyle of Lochalsh 3C 4
Lewis 3A 5
Mull 3D 4
Oban 3D 4
Orkney 1A 5
Perth 2D 5
Prestwick Airport 3E 4
Scone Palace 2D 5
Shetland Islands 1B 5
Skye 3B 4
Sterling 3E 5
Stornoway 3A 4
Stranrear 3B 6
Thurso 2A 5
Tobermory 3C 4
Ullapool 3B 5
Serbia
Beograd 3A 40
Nis 3C 41
Novi Sad A3 41
Uzice 3B 41
Sicily (Italy)
Agrigento 2D 26
Cefalu 2D 26
Marsala 1C 26
Mazara 2D 26
Messina 3D 26
Mount Etna 3D 26
Palermo 2C 26

Syracusa 3E 26
Trapani 2C 26
Slovakia
Bratislava 3B 38
Kosice 2B 39
Presov 2A 39
Spis Castle 2A 39
Trencin 3A 38
Zilina 3A 39
Zvolen 3B 39
Slovenia
Bled Jezero 2B 61
Koper 3D 61
Ljubljana 1D 38
Ljubljana 2C 61
Maribor 2C 38
Piran 3D 61
Skocjan Caves 3D 61
Spain
Alacant 2C 19
Albacete L. L. 3C 19
Alcazar de San Juan 3B 19
Alcudia (Palmer) 3E 12
Algeciras (UK) 2D 18
Alhama de Murcia 3C 19
Almeria 3D 19
Antequera 3D 18
Arevalo 3D 16
Astorga 3B 16
Avila 3D 16
Badajoz 2B 18
Barcelona 1B 19
Benidorm 2C 19
Bilbao 3B 17
Burgos 3C 17
Cabez del Buey 3B 18
Caceras 2E 16
Cadiz 2D 18
Calaf 2D 12
Canfranc 2B 12
Castell de Bellver (Palma) 3E 12
Ceuta 2D 18
Ciudad Real 3B 18
Ciudad Rodrigo 3D 16
Costa Verde 3A 16
Cuenca 1D 12

Denia 2E 12
Don Benito 3B 18
Eivissa 3B 14
Ferrol 2A 16
Formentera 1D 19
Gelida 3D 12
Gibraltar (UK) 2D 18
Granada 3D 18
Huelva 2C 18
Huesca 2B 12
Ibiza 1C 19
Irun 2A 12
Jaen 3C 18
Jerez de los Cabelleros 2B 18
Jerez Frontera 2C 18
La Coruna 2A 16
La Pobla de Segur 2C 12
Leon 3B 16
Linares 3C 19
Lleida 2E 17
Logrono 1B 12
Lugo 2B 16
Madrid 3A 19
Manresa 2D 12
Marbella 2D 18
Medina del Campo 3C 16
Merida 2B 18
Minorca 3E 13
Monforte de Lemos 2B 16
Montserrat 2D 12
Murcia del Carmen 2C 19
Orihuela 2C 19
Ourense 2B 16
Oviedo 3A 16
Palencia 3C 16
Palma 3B 14
Palma del Rio 3C 18
Plasencia Ciudad 3A 18
Pontevedra 2B 16
Port Bou 3C 12
Puebla de Sanabria 3B 16
Puigcerda 3C 12
Requena Utiel 2E 12
Ronda 2D 18
Sahagun 3B 16
Salamanca 3D 16

San Lorenzo 3A 19
Santander 3B 17
Santiago de Compostela 2A 16
Segovia 3D 17
Sevilla 2C 18
Soria 1B 12
Tarragona 1B 19
Toledo 3B 19
Ubeda 3C 19
Valencia 2C 19
Valliloilid 3C 16
Vigo Guixar 2B 16
Villena 2C 19
Vitoria 1A 12
Xativa 2E 12
Zamora 3C 16
Zaragoza 2D 17
Sweden
Aare 3B 33
Aland 3C 30
Arvidsjaur 3D 28
Boden 3D 28
Borgholm Castle 2E 30
Bornholm 3D 35
Duved 1B 30
Falun 2C 30
Gallivare 3C 28
Goteborg 3B 34
Gotland 2B 35
Halmstad 1E 30
Harnosand 3B 30
Ice Hotel 3C 28
Kalmar 2E 30
Karlskrona 2E 30
Kiruna 3C 28
Mora 2C 30
Nassjo 2E 30
Northern Lights 2B 28
Nykoping 3D 30
Nynashamn 3D 30
Orebro 2D 30
Ostersund 2B 30
Skelleftea 3E 28
Soderhamn 3C 30
Stockholm 2E 33
Sundsvall 3B 30
Varberg 1E 30
Visby 2B 35

Switzerland
Andermatt 2A 51
Arosa 2E 52
Basel 2B 48
Bellinzona 1C 51
Bern 1B 22
Bern 2D 48
Brig 2C 22
Champery 2C 50
Chillion Castle 2B 50
Chur 1D 49
Chur 3C 22
Davos 2E 54
Geneve 1B 50
Grindelwald 3A 51
Gruyeres 2A 50
Interlaken 3A 51
Jungfraujoch 3B 51
Lausanne 2A 50
Lepontine Alps 2B 51
Locarno 1C 51
Lugano 1C 51
Luzern 3C 49
Martigny 3C 50
Matterhorn 3C 51
Montreux 2B 50
Murten 2D 48
Mustair 3A 54
Olten 3B 48
Pontresina 2B 54
Rapperswil 2C 49
Rigi Bahnen 3C 49
Romont 2A 50
Schaffhausen 3A 49
Sion 3B 50
St Gallen 1B 49
St Moritz 2A 54
Thun 3D 48
Top of Europe 3B 51
Verbier 3C 50
Wil 2B 49
Winterthur 2B 49
Zermatt 3C 51
Zurich 2B 22
Zurich 3B 49
T
Tunisia
Bizerte 2E 15
Enfidha 1E 26
Sousse 1E 26

Tunis 1D 26
Turkey
Afyonkarahisar 1B 47
Alacati 3B 47
Antalya 1D 47
Assos 3E 45
Bandirma 2D 45
Bodrum 3D 47
Bursa 1D 45
Canakkale 3D 45
Cesme 3B 47
Chimeara 1D 47
Ephesus 3C 47
Eskisehir 1A 47
Gallipoli 3D 45
Halkali 1C 45
Isparta 1C 47
Istanbul 1C 45
Izmir 3B 47
Kapikale 3B 45
Marmaris 2D 47
Pendik 1C 45
Pergamon 2E 45
U
Ukraine
Brest 2E 66
W
Wales (UK)
Aberystwyth 3A 8
Blaenau Ffestiniog 3D 6
Caerphilly 3B 8
Cardigan Bay 2A 8
Cardiff 3B 8
Chepstow 3B 8
Conway 3D 6
Fishguard 2A 8
Harlech 3E 6
Holyhead 2C 6
Holy Island 2C 6
Pembroke 2B 8
Portmeirion 3D 6
Snowdonia 3D 6
Swansea 2B 8
Tenby 2B 8

Euro Currencies

Country	Currency
Albania	ALL Leke
Algeria	BZD Dinas
Austria	EUR Euro
Belarus	BYN Ruble
Belgium	EUR Euro
Bosnia	BAM Mark
Bulgaria	BGN Leva
Croatia	JRK Kuna
Czechia	CZK Koruna
Denmark	DKK Drone
Estonia	EUR Euro
Finland	EUR Euro
France	EUR Euro
Germany	EUR Euro
Greece	EUR Euro
Hungary	CZK Koruna
Ireland	EUR Euro
Italy	EUR Euro
Latvia	EUR Euro
Lithuania	LTL Litai
Luxembourg	EUR Euro
Macedonia	MKD Denar
Montenegro	EUR Euro
Morocco	MAD Dirham
Netherlands	EUR Euro
Norway	NOK Kroner
Poland	PLN Zloty
Portugal	EUR Euro
Romania	RON Leu
Russia	RUB Ruble
Serbia	RSD Dinar
Slovakia	EUR Euro
Slovenia	EUR Euro
Spain	EUR Euro
Sweden	SEK Krona
Switzerland	CHR Franc
Tunisia	TND Dinas
Turkey	TRY Lira
Ukraine	UAH
UK	GPD Pound